2 Hour
Book
of
Mormon

A
Book of Mormon
Primer

2 Hour
Book
of
Mormon

A
Book of Mormon
Primer

by

Larry Anderson Ph.D

ISBN: 1-55517-481-7
v.2

Published by Bonneville Books

Distributed by:
925 North Main, Springville, UT 84663 • 801/489-4084

CFI Distribution • CFI Books • Council Press • Bonneville Books

Typeset by Virginia Reeder
Cover design by Adam Ford
Cover design © 2000 by Lyle Mortimer

Printed in the United States of America

Preface

Adults start here:

This book is a condensed version of the Book of Mormon. The vocabulary is somewhat simpler. An above average reader can complete it in a few hours. Most take longer. Many readers report that they "couldn't put it down."

In addition to focusing on fundamental teachings, this book presents somewhat less violence and explicitness. Some advanced doctrinal writings, such as the prophecies of Isaiah, are also not extensively included. Still, every effort was made to avoid changing, adding to, or diminishing Book of Mormon teachings.

I hope this book leads you to study and cherish the Book of Mormon.

Young readers start here:

Scriptures are God's words written in books. The Book of Mormon is scripture. This book is not the Book of Mormon. This book tells many stories and ideas that are in the Book of Mormon.

One way this book is different from the Book of Mormon is that this book is easier to read. This book does not have all the words and stories of the Book of Mormon.

After you read this book, read the Book of Mormon. Think and pray about it, too. If you do, God will show you in your heart and mind that the Book of Mormon is true.

Foreword
from the
Book of Mormon

The Book of Mormon tells wonderful things the Lord has done for people. It tells that Jesus is our Eternal God. It tells us God shows himself to all nations.

The Book of Mormon is a history of the people who lived in the Americas long ago. Prophets wrote their stories in books with metal pages. The Book of Mormon was written on gold pages. When the book was finished, God told the prophet Moroni to hide it in a hill in the farm land of New York.

Many years later, God led a young man named Joseph Smith to the book. The words were in a language Joseph Smith could not understand. God helped Joseph read and write the words into English.

The angel Moroni showed the gold plates to three men. They were Oliver Cowdery, David Whitmer and Martin Harris.

These three men said:

An angel of God came and showed us the book made from gold. We touched the pages and saw the writings. God told us that the Book of Mormon is true. We promise you this is what we saw and heard. The honor goes to the Father, and to the Son, and to the Holy Ghost, which is one God. Amen.

Joseph Smith showed the gold plates to eight other men. They are: Christian Whitmer, Jacob Whitmer, Jr., John Whitmer, Hiram Page, Joseph Smith, Sr., Hyrum Smith, and Samuel H. Smith.

These eight men said:

Joseph Smith showed us the book made of gold. We held it and turned the metal pages. We promise that Joseph Smith showed us the gold book. God knows we saw it.

FIRST NEPHI
Son of Lehi

1st Nephi 1

I am Nephi, a young man. My parents taught me well. Our family had hard times, but God blessed us greatly. Many years ago my father, Lehi, lived in Jerusalem. He was one of God's prophets. He told the people they must repent, or God would destroy them.

My father loved the people. He prayed to the Lord for them. The Lord came to Lehi and showed him many things about the people. The things Lehi saw made him shake and tremble. He was so upset he laid on his bed in sadness.

While Lehi was resting, he saw a vision of heaven. He saw God sitting on his throne with many angels singing praise to him. One angel was the brightest. He was brighter than the sun. Twelve others followed him.

These angels came down to the earth to my father and gave him a book. As Lehi read it, he felt the wonderful Spirit of the Lord. The book said Jerusalem would be destroyed and many people would be slaves.

Because of the things the Lord showed to him, Lehi was filled with joy. Lehi said: Great and amazing are your works, O Lord God Almighty! You are merciful. You will not allow those who come to you to perish!

Lehi went to the people and told them the things the Lord showed him about Jerusalem. He told the people that Jesus would one day come to save them. But the Jews yelled at Lehi. They did not want to hear about their sins. The Jews were angry with Lehi. They tried to kill him, but the Lord protected Lehi.

1st Nephi 2

The Lord told my father to move to the wilderness. Lehi left his house and land and his gold and silver. He took his family with supplies and tents into a desert. My mother, Sariah, and my older brothers, Laman, Lemuel and Sam and I went with him. After we traveled three days, we put up our tents by a river that went to the sea.

Lehi spoke to my brother, Laman, saying: I wish you would be like this river, always running into the fountain of good! He also spoke to my brother, Lemuel, saying: I wish you would be like this valley, firm in keeping the commandments of the Lord!

Laman and Lemuel were stubborn. They complained a lot. They believed we lost our land and gold and silver and fancy things just to go die in the wilderness. They said it was Lehi's fault; they said he was foolish. They did not understand the ways of God. They thought the strong city, Jerusalem, could not be destroyed.

Laman and Lemuel tried to kill my father, but my father spoke to them with the power of the Holy Spirit. They became so frightened that they began to shake. Lehi's power was so strong they were afraid to fight him.

I, Nephi, was young, but I was curious to know the mysteries of God. When I prayed, the Lord spoke to me by his Holy Spirit. He softened my heart to help me believe my father's words.

I did not rebel against my father. I told my younger brother Sam what the Lord had told me. Sam believed me, but Laman and Lemuel would not listen.

The Lord said to me: You are blessed, Nephi, because of your faith. You have searched for me with an open heart. If you keep my commandments, you will do well. You will be led to a special land I prepared for you that is better than all other lands.

You will be ruler and teacher over your brothers. If they

fight against me, I will curse them with a painful curse. They will have no power over your people.

But if your people fight me, Laman and Lemuel's people will attack your people. This will help your people remember my power and promises.

1st Nephi 3

My father told me the Lord wanted me and my brothers to return to Jerusalem to get the books of the Jews [parts of the Old Testament].

Lehi said: Your brothers complain and say it is too dangerous to go back and get the book; but this is the Lord's commandment. So go, Nephi, and the Lord will help you, because you do not complain.

I, Nephi, told my father I would go and do the things that the Lord commands. I know God only gives commandments that he prepares a way for us to do it.

So Laman, Lemuel, Sam and Nephi went to Jerusalem to get the books from a strong man named Laban. First Laman went to Laban's house and talked with him. He asked Laban for the books made of brass.

Laban became angry and threw Laman out of his house. He called Laman a robber and tried to kill him. My brother ran back to us and told us what Laban had done. We became sad. My brothers wanted to go back to our father in the wilderness.

I said to them: We will not go back to our father until we have finished the Lord's command. God is wise and knows we will need these books to teach our children the holy prophets' words. From the beginning of man to this day, God has told prophets to write his words in books.

We will go to our father's old home where he left all his riches. We will trade our gold and silver to Laban for the brass books. We took our gold and silver to Laban. We told him we would give him all our riches if he would give us the brass books.

When Laban saw our many riches, he wanted to steal them.

He threw us out and sent his servants to kill us. We ran away and left our riches behind. We ran until we were out of Jerusalem. We hid in a cave.

Laman and Lemuel were angry with Sam and I. They said hard words to us and hit us with a stick.

As they were hitting us with a stick, an angel of the Lord came and spoke to them, saying: Why do you hit your younger brothers? The Lord chose Nephi to rule you because of your sins. Go back to Jerusalem; the Lord will put Laban in your hands.

After the angel left, Laman and Lemuel complained again, saying: How is it possible for the Lord to put Laban into our hands? Laban is a mighty man. He has fifty warriors. We are not strong enough to stop them.

1st Nephi 4

I said: Let us go back to Jerusalem. Let us be faithful in keeping God's commandments. God is mightier than Laban even if Laban had ten thousand warriors.

Let us be strong like Moses. He parted the Red Sea. The Israelites walked on dry ground while Pharaoh's mighty armies drowned. How can you doubt? An angel spoke to you. Let us go. The Lord will help us.

Although my brothers were angry and kept complaining, they followed me back to the city walls. It was dark at night. My brothers hid outside the wall while I sneaked in the city and went towards Laban's house. I did not know what to do.

The Holy Spirit guided me to a man lying on the ground. I could see it was Laban. He was drunk. The Holy Spirit told me to kill him. I did not want to but I did.

I put on Laban's coat and armor and went to Laban's treasure house. A servant there had the keys to the treasure. Because it was dark and because he saw Laban's clothes and sword, the servant thought I was Laban. I ordered him in Laban's voice to come with me to the treasure house.

I told him to carry the brass books to my brothers. He

thought I was Laban and that I was talking about the brothers of the church. He obeyed and followed me.

When my brothers saw me, they were frightened. They thought I was Laban and that he had killed me and had come to kill them. They started to run away.

I called out to them. They recognized my voice and stopped running. Then the servant of Laban became scared. Now he knew I was not Laban.

He was about to run back to the city, but I am large and strong. I grabbed him, whose name was Zoram, and held him. We wanted him to stay with us so the Jews would not find out about us. They would surely chase and kill us.

I told Zoram that if he would listen to my words, we would let him live. I promised him he need not fear. If he would come with us, he would be a free man. I said to him: The Lord told us to do this. If you come to the wilderness with us, you can live with us.

Zoram got courage from my words. He promised to come with us to our father. He promised he would live with us. When Zoram made his promise to us, our fears about him stopped. We took the plates of brass and walked back to the desert.

1st Nephi 5

When we returned, our father was filled with joy. My mother, Sariah, was glad. She thought we died in the wilderness. She had complained against my father; she called him a dreamer. She told him: You have led us out from our home and people, now my sons are gone and we are going to die in the wilderness.

My father tried to comfort Sariah. He said to her: I know I am a visionary man. But I know the goodness of God, because of my visions. The Lord will save our sons from Laban and bring them back to us. So when we returned, their joy was full. We all gave thanks to God.

My father read the brass books from start to end. They had

the five books of Moses, which told the story of the creation of the world and of Adam and Eve.

The books also had history of the Jews from the beginning down to the time of Zedekiah, king of Judah. The plates also told the prophecies of the holy prophets.

When my father saw these things, he was filled with the Spirit. He began to prophesy that these brass books [parts of the Old Testament] would go to all nations. They were of great worth to us; they have the word of the Lord.

1st Nephi 7

The Lord told my father we should not go alone into the wilderness. My brothers and I should return to Jerusalem and bring Ishmael and his family into the wilderness. When we went to Ishmael's family, the Lord softened their hearts. They came with us to the wilderness.

But as we traveled back to my father's tent, Laman, Lemuel and two of Ishmael's daughters and two of his sons changed their minds. They got homesick and wanted to go back to Jerusalem.

I said to Laman and Lemuel: You are my older brothers. Why are you so hard in your hearts and so blind in your minds? Why must I, your younger brother, set an example for you?

Have you forgotten that you have seen an angel of the Lord? Have you forgotten the great things the Lord has done for us? He saved us from the hands of Laban! Have you forgotten the Lord is able to do all things for people if they show faith in him?

Let us be faithful to him; he will lead us to a wonderful land. The Lord told our father Jerusalem would soon be destroyed. Do not go back.

If you go back, you will be destroyed, too. The choice is yours, but remember the words I speak to you. If you go, you will die. The Lord's Spirit tells me so.

When I said these words to my brothers, they tried to kill me. They grabbed me and tied my hands and feet. They were going to leave me in the desert to be eaten by wild animals.

I prayed to the Lord: O Lord, by my faith that is in you, save me from my brothers. Give me strength to break these ropes. When I said these words, the ropes came off and I stood up before my brothers.

I spoke to them again. This made them even more angry. They tried to grab me again, but some of Ishmael's family talked to my brothers and softened their hearts.

Laman and Lemuel became filled with sorrow because of their sins. They bowed down to me and begged me to forgive them. I forgave them and I told them to pray, not to me, but to God, for forgiveness. When we arrived at my father's tent, we all gave thanks to the Lord.

1st Nephi 8

My father, Lehi, said to us: I have dreamed a dream; I have seen a vision. I have joy in the Lord because of Nephi and of Sam. I believe they and many of their children will be saved. But I fear for Laman and Lemuel.

I saw in my dream a man dressed in a white robe. He asked me to follow him. He took me to a dark and dreary wasteland. After many hours in darkness, I prayed to the Lord to have mercy on me.

Then I saw a large field and a tree with fruit that can make you happy. I tasted the fruit and it was more sweet and delicious than anything I had ever tasted. It filled my soul with great joy. It was the most wonderful fruit.

I wanted my family to have some. I looked around to see if my family was there. I looked around and I saw Sariah, Sam and Nephi. They stood not knowing which way to go.

I called to them in a loud voice to come and eat the sweet fruit. They came and ate. I also wanted Laman and Lemuel to come and eat the fruit, but they would not come.

I saw a dirty river. I also saw a straight and narrow path leading to the tree. Beside the path, an iron rod [handrail] stretched to the tree.

Crowds of people walked forward to reach the path that led to the tree. When they started on the path to the tree, a dark mist rose up in their way. The cloudy mist was so thick and dark that many people could not find their way. They wandered off and were lost. Others pressed forward, grabbed the iron rod and held on until they made it to the tree.

On the other side of the river was a large building. It was filled with men and women, both old and young. They were wearing fancy clothes. They were teasing and pointing fingers at the people who came to eat the fruit.

We did not listen to them. But the people who did listen to them looked around and became ashamed. They walked away into evil paths and were lost. Others came forward holding tight to the iron rod until they came to the tree and ate its fruit.

Laman and Lemuel did not eat the fruit. Lehi feared they would fall away from the Lord. He urged them with all the feelings of a tender parent to hear his words. After he asked them to keep the commandments of the Lord, he stopped preaching to them.

1st Nephi 9

My father's many visions are not written on these plates. These are not the plates with a full history of my people. These plates are more for ministry; the other plates are more of history.

I do not know the purposes of these plates, only that God commanded me to write them. The Lord knows all things and prepares his works. And thus it is. Amen.

1st Nephi 10

After his dream, my father spoke to us about the Jews. He told us the great city of Jerusalem would be destroyed. Many of the

Jews would be taken away as slaves. He said the Jews would one day be let free and return to their land.

Lehi said that six hundred years from the time we left Jerusalem, God would raise up Jesus Christ to be the Savior of the world. Lehi said a prophet would baptize Jesus in the Jordan River. Lehi said the Jews would kill Jesus, but Jesus would come alive again and show himself to many people by the Holy Ghost.

1st Nephi 11

By the Holy Ghost's power, the Lord will tell these things to anyone who seeks him. I believed the Lord would be able to show them to me. One day, when I sat thinking in my heart about the things my father had seen, the Holy Spirit took me to a high mountain.

The Spirit spoke to me as a person talks with another. The Spirit asked me: What do you want? I answered: I want to see the things that my father saw. The Spirit said: Do you believe your father saw the tree with the good fruit? I said: Yes, I believe all my father's words.

When I said this, the Spirit shouted with a loud voice: Hosanna to the Lord, the most high God. God is ruler over all the earth, even above all. You are blessed, Nephi, because you believe in the Son of the most high God.

You will see the things you asked about. After you have seen the tree with the fruit that your father tasted, you will also see a man come down out of heaven. After you have seen him, you will know that he is God's Son.

Then I looked and saw a tree. It was like the tree my father had seen. Its beauty was far beyond all beauty. Its whiteness was whiter than falling snow. The angel asked: Do you know the meaning of the tree that your father saw? I answered: Yes, the tree represents God's love. It is most desirable above all things.

Then I saw that the iron rod was God's word that leads to the fountain of living waters and to the tree of life.

The angel said: The river of filthy water represents hell. The mists of darkness are the devil's temptations. The devil blinds the eyes, hardens the hearts and leads people away to wide roads where they become lost.

The large building is pride. A great and terrible canyon divides the people in the building from the people at the tree. This canyon is the justice of the Eternal God.

Then I saw the great city of Jerusalem and other cities. I saw the city of Nazareth. In Nazareth, I saw a young woman. The angel said to me: The woman who you see will be the mother of God's Son. I saw the woman holding a child in her arms.

The angel said to me: See Jesus Christ, the Son of the Eternal Father! I looked and I saw God's Son going among people. I saw many kneel at his feet and worship him. I saw He was the Savior of the world.

People gathered to hear Him. He taught the people with power and glory. I saw twelve men following Him; the angel called them apostles. I saw many people who were sick with all kinds of illness. They were healed by the power of Jesus Christ.

I saw the people take Jesus Christ. They lifted Him up on a cross. He let them kill Him so he could pay for people's sins.

I saw people gathered to fight the Lord's apostles. Crowds were gathered in a large building, like the building that my father saw. The angel of the Lord spoke to me again, saying: This is the world and its wisdom gathered to fight against the twelve apostles.

Then the large building collapsed. The fall was terrible. The angel said: Terrible will be the fall of all people who fight against the Lord's twelve apostles.

1st Nephi 12

The angel said: See your children and grandchildren. See the children of Laman and Lemuel. I saw the Promised Land [Americas] with many cities and people. I saw armies gathered to battle and many wars among them.

I saw a mist of darkness there. I saw lightning and heard thunder. There were earthquakes and violent noises. I saw the ground and rocks break apart. I saw mountains tumbling to pieces. Many cities were sunk; many cities were burned with fire; many cities crumbled to the ground.

I saw many people who did not fall. The heavens opened and Jesus Christ came down. He showed himself to them. I saw the Holy Ghost come to twelve other apostles chosen by God.

Because of my people's pride, I saw Laman's and Lemuel's people fight and kill my people. At last, all my people were killed. My brothers' people became many, but they were full of sin.

1st Nephi 13

I saw many strong nations [Europe] that lived across the [Atlantic] ocean. The angel said to me: These are the nations of the Gentiles. I saw their gold, silver, silks and fine clothes. Many of the Gentile people were kept poor by the rich nations.

The Spirit of God will lead a Gentile man [Columbus] to sail across the ocean to the Promised Land where my brothers' people live. The Spirit of God will also tell other Gentiles to leave their nations and go across the ocean.

I saw many groups of Gentiles [pilgrims and immigrants] come to the Promised Land [Americas]. By the power of God, many people will come to this land which is better than all other lands.

I saw God's anger was on my brothers' people [the Indians] because of their sins. Because of their sins, the Promised Land will be given to the Gentiles. My brothers' people [the Indians] will be scattered and killed. I saw the Spirit of the Lord on the new people. They grew strong.

I, Nephi, saw that the people who came across the ocean would humble themselves to the Lord. The power of the Lord was with them. Then I saw their mother nation [England] come to battle against them [Revolutionary War]. But God's power was with the people and God's anger was on anyone who fought against them.

The people [pilgrims and immigrants] who left the evil Gentile nations [Europe] carried a book with them [the Bible]. The angel said: This book is a history of the Jews.

It tells the promises the Lord made to the people of Israel. It also has many prophecies. It is like the brass books that you got from Laban. This book [Bible] is of great worth.

The angel said: when the book comes from the Jews, it will have the whole gospel of the Lord. But after it leaves the hand of the twelve apostles, many of the plain gospel parts will be taken out of the book. Many of the Lord's promises to the people of Israel will be taken out, too.

Evil leaders of the Gentile's great church will do this so they can get power over their members. After these plain parts are taken away, the book [Bible] will go to all the nations. But because of the things that are taken out, many people will stumble.

The Lord will not allow the Gentiles to always stay blind to Jesus' gospel. He will not allow the Gentiles to kill all your brothers' people [Indians]. After Jesus Christ visits the Jews in Israel, he will visit your people [in the Americas].

In the last days, the Gentiles will punish your brothers' people [Indians]. The Gentiles will stumble because many of the plain parts of the gospel are kept from them by that awful church. But the Lord will show his mercy. In his own way, he will bring to them much of his gospel.

He will bring many of the things that you and your people will write [Book of Mormon] to the world. Even though your people will be destroyed and your brothers' people will shrink in unbelief, the things you write [Book of Mormon] will be brought by the gift and power of the Lamb. In this way, the gospel of Jesus Christ will be brought again to all the world.

Blessed are those who seek to bring forth Zion at that day. They will have the gift and power of the Holy Ghost. If they stay true to the end, they will be saved in the kingdom of God.

Then I saw the book that my offspring will write [Book of

Mormon] and the book that the Jews will write [Bible] come to my brothers' people [the Indians].

After these books came to them, I saw other books [Doctrine and Covenants, Pearl of Great Price] that came from the Gentiles by the power of God. They will convince all people that the books of the prophets [Old Testament] and of the twelve apostles [New Testament] are true.

The angel said: These books will show the truth of the book of the Jews [Bible] and will teach the plain and important things that have been taken away.

They will join together in one. There is one God and one Shepherd over all the earth. The books will show all nations and people that Jesus Christ is the Son of the Eternal Father. All people must come to Jesus to be saved.

1st Nephi 14

If the Gentiles listen to Jesus Christ, He will show Himself to them in word, in power and in action to take away their stumbling blocks. If they soften their hearts toward Jesus Christ, they will be a blessed people in the Promised Land forever.

Jesus Christ will do a great and amazing work. It will lead many people to peace and life eternal. But those who are hard in their hearts and blind in their minds will be brought to prison and destruction.

The angel said: There are only two churches. One is the church of Jesus Christ; the other is the church of the devil. Whoever does not belong to the church of Jesus Christ will belong to that other church. The awful church ruled across many seas. It had power over all the earth.

Then I saw those of the church of Jesus Christ who were the saints of God. They were also on all the face of the earth. But their numbers were few and their power on the earth was small.

I saw a man dressed in a white robe. The angel said: See John, one of the twelve apostles. He will see and write about the end of the world. The things he will write are true. They will be written in the Bible.

God has shown all things to other people. Those writings are sealed up, but they will come when the Lord is ready. I, Nephi, write only a small part of the things that I saw, but I am not allowed to write the rest.

1st Nephi 15

After my vision, I returned to the tent of my father. My brothers were arguing with each other. At first I was too tired to talk with them. When I had strength, I asked them why they were arguing. They said: We cannot understand our father's words.

I asked them: Have you prayed to the Lord? They said to me: We have not. I said: Our father said these things are hard to understand unless you ask the Lord. The Lord has said if we ask Him in faith, He will give it to us.

They asked me: What is the tree our father saw in the dream? I said to them: It is the tree of life. They asked: What is the iron rod that leads to the tree? I said: The iron rod is the word of God. Whoever listens to God's word and holds to it will never weaken.

They asked: What is the river? I said: The water in the river represents evil. The river is like a wide canyon that keeps wicked people away from the tree of life. The justice of God will divide the evil people from the good.

The day will come when we will be judged for our actions. If our actions have been evil, we cannot live in the kingdom of God. Nothing evil can enter God's kingdom.

1st Nephi 16

My brothers said to me: You have said hard things against us. We cannot stand it. I told them that truth is hard only for the guilty. It cuts to the heart. Then Laman and Lemuel humbled themselves before the Lord. I had joy and great hope in them.

I married one of Ishmael's daughters. Laman and Lemuel also married his daughters. Zoram married Ishmael's oldest daughter.

The Lord's voice came to my father in the night telling him to move further into the desert. In the morning, my father arose and went to the tent door. He saw a strange round brass ball on the ground. Inside the ball were two pointers. It pointed the way we should go.

We traveled for many days, hunting food with bows, arrows, stones and slings. We followed the directions of the compass ball. It led us to the greener parts of the land.

One day my steel bow broke. I had to return without food to our tired and hungry families. Laman, Lemuel and Ishmael's sons began to complain against the Lord. Even my father, Lehi, began to complain against the Lord.

Because my bow broke and my brothers' bows lost their spring, it was hard to find food. I made a bow out of wood and an arrow out of a straight stick. I asked my father: Where should I go to get food? He prayed carefully, for my father was truly sorry he complained against God.

The Lord's voice came to my father telling him to look on the compass. I learned that the pointers in the compass worked by faith and obedience.

The compass led me to the top of a mountain. I found wild animals. When I returned with the meat, our joy was so great! We were humble before the Lord and gave thanks to him. Through small things, the Lord can bring about great joy.

After we traveled for many more days, Ishmael died. His daughters became sad and complained against my father. They cried out: Our father is dead. We have wandered too much in the desert. We have suffered hunger and thirst. We are worn out. We want to go back to Jerusalem.

Laman said: Let us kill Lehi and Nephi. Nephi says the Lord and angels have talked to him. We know he lies to us. He does miracles by sneaky tricks to fool our eyes. Maybe he wants to lead us to some strange wilderness and make himself king over us.

The Lord's voice came again and scolded them greatly. They repented of their sins and the Lord blessed us with food again so we would not die.

1st Nephi 17

We traveled in hardship. Our wives gave birth in the wilderness. My parents had two more sons; the older was called Jacob and the younger Joseph.

The Lord did not allow us to use much fire. The Lord told us: You do not need to cook your meat; I will make it sweet for you.

Our women had plenty of milk for their children. Our wives became strong like men. We lived and traveled in the desert for eight years.

At last we came to a large sea. We pitched our tents by the shore. Even though we had suffered much we cannot write it all we were happy. The land had much fruit and wild honey, we called the place Bountiful. We learned that if we keep the commandments, God will help and strengthen us. He will provide a way to do what he asks of us.

One day I was on a mountain praying. The Lord said to me: You must build a ship so I may carry your people across the seas. I asked the Lord: Where will I go to find metal ore to make tools? The Lord told me where to go to find ore to make tools. I made a bellows from the skins of animals to blow the fire. Then I made tools from the ore.

When my brothers saw I was going to build a ship, they began to complain against me. They said: Our brother is a fool. He thinks he can build a ship. He thinks he can cross the great seas. They did not believe I could build a ship. They did not believe the Lord taught me, so they would not help me.

I became sad because of the hardness of their hearts. When they saw I was sad, they became happy. They made fun of me and said: We knew you could not build a ship. We knew you do not have good sense. You are like our father, led by foolish ideas. You let us suffer many years in the wilderness, when we could have enjoyed life back in our home. We could have been happy.

Then I, Nephi, said to them: You are slow to remember your God but quick to sin. The Lord told our father to go into the wilderness. You have seen an angel. He spoke to you in a still small voice, but you were past feeling. He spoke to you in a voice of thunder that made the earth shake. But you are still hard in your hearts. My soul is full of sorrow for you. I fear you will be thrown off forever.

When I spoke these words, my brothers were angry with me and wanted to throw me into the sea. As they came to grab me, I said to them: Stop. I am full of the Spirit of God, even so my body has no strength. In the name of the Almighty God, I command you to not touch me. God will destroy anyone who touches me.

I told them God told me to build a ship. Whatever God tells me to do, I can do it. If he commands me to say to this water to be dirt, then it would be dirt. I also told them to stop complaining against our father and to help me build the ship.

They did not dare touch me for many days. Then the Lord said to me: Reach your hand out and touch your brothers. I will shock them, so they will know that I am the Lord their God.

So I stretched my hand to my brothers and the Lord shocked them. They said: We know the Lord is with you, for we know it is the power of the Lord that shakes us.

They fell down before me and were about to worship me, but I did not allow them. I said: I am your brother. Worship only the Lord your God and honor your father and your mother.

1st Nephi 18

I often went to the mountain to pray. The Lord showed me great things. He showed me strange ways to work wood for the ship. When the ship was finished, my brothers saw it was very strong.

The Lord told my father to move into the ship. The next day we took much fruit, meat and honey. We went into the ship with our wives and our children. We sailed out to sea in the ship and we were driven by the wind towards the Promised Land.

After many days, my brothers and the sons of Ishmael and their wives began to make merry dancing, singing and speaking with rudeness. I feared the Lord would be angry and let us be swallowed up in the sea.

I spoke to them, but they were angry. They said: We will not allow our younger brother to rule us. Laman and Lemuel tied me with ropes and treated me meanly.

The Lord allowed this to happen to show his power. After they tied me up, the compass stopped working. They did not know where to guide the ship.

A terrible storm started. It drove us backward for three days. My brothers began to think they would be drowned, but they would not untie me.

My father, Lehi, said many things to them, but they threatened anyone who pleaded for me. My parents went to their sickbeds. They were near death with sorrow. Their gray hairs were about to be brought down and all of us go to a watery grave.

Even the tears and prayers of my wife and my children did not soften the hearts of my brothers. But on the fourth day, the storm became even more dangerous. Our ship began to sink.

My brothers began to see that God's anger was on them. They must repent or be drowned. Only the power of God, which threatened to swallow them up in the sea, would scare them. At last, they untied me.

I thanked God all day long. My wrists and ankles were sore and swollen, but I did not complain against the Lord because of my pain.

When I prayed to the Lord, the winds and storm stopped. There was a great calm. I held the compass and it worked for me.

We sailed for days and finally came to the Promised Land. We all thanked the Lord for sparing us and leading us. We pitched our tents and began to farm the ground. We planted our seeds and they grew fast and plentiful.

We went into the forests and found cows, oxen, horses, goats, donkeys and all kinds of wild animals. We found all kinds of gold, silver and copper ore.

1st Nephi 19

The Lord told me to make metal plates to write a history of my people. I made the metal plates from gold. If I write any mistakes, the weakness is in me not in the truth. The things that some people think are of great worth, others will trample under their feet.

An angel said Jesus will come in six hundred years from the time my father left Jerusalem. The people will trample him under their feet, spit on Him and beat Him. He will allow them to do it, because of His loving kindness for all people.

They will send Jesus into the hands of evil men to be crucified and killed. His body will be placed in a tomb and there will be three days of darkness. This will be a sign of His death to those who live all around the world.

For the prophet said: The Lord God will visit all the people of Israel on that day. He will visit some with his voice and he will bring them great joy. He will visit others with thunder and lightning, by storm, fire, smoke, darkness, by the opening of the earth and by mountains that will be carried up. The rocks of the earth will tear apart as a sign that Jesus is God's Son.

Because the Jews will crucify the God of Israel, people will hurt the Jews. Because they turn their hearts away and hate the Holy One of Israel, the Jews will wander, die and be hated.

The day will come when the Jews will turn their hearts to the Holy One of Israel; then God will remember them. God will remember the islands of the sea. He will gather in all the people who are of the people of Israel.

1st Nephi 20-22

After I, Nephi, read the things written on the brass plates, my brothers asked me: What do these things mean? I answered: It appears the people of Israel will sooner or later be scattered all over the earth and among all nations.

The greater part of the tribes have been led away. They are scattered here and there and on the islands of the sea. The Jews will be scattered and hated, because they will harden their hearts against the Lord.

The Lord God will raise up a mighty nation among the Gentiles [Americans] on the face of this land [Americas]. They will scatter our people [the Indians]. Then God will do a wonderful work among the Gentiles. It will be of great worth to our people and to all Israel.

The time will come when churches try to get gain and power over people. The churches will try to become popular and seek things of the world. They will fear and tremble.

But the righteous will not be destroyed. The time will come when all who fight against Zion will be cut off. The Lord will prepare a way for his people. He will raise up a prophet like Moses of old. All who will not hear that prophet will be cut off from among the people.

Jesus will gather his children from all over the earth. He knows his sheep and they know him. There will be one flock and one shepherd. He feeds his sheep and they find pasture in him.

I, Nephi, say that all these things must happen. The words on the plates of brass are true. They teach that people should obey God's commandments. If you will obey his commandments and hang on to the end, you will be saved.

SECOND NEPHI
Son of Lehi

2nd Nephi 1

After I ended teaching my brothers, our father, Lehi, spoke to Laman and Lemuel. He spoke about the great things the Lord did for them. He told them about their rebellions on the waters and God's mercies in sparing them.

He spoke to them about the Promised Land, a land that is better than all other lands. As long as they obey the Lord, this land will be a land of liberty.

God kept this land hidden from other nations. If not, many nations would overrun the land. If we keep the commandments, we will grow here and we will be kept secret from other nations.

The time will come when our people will shrink in unbelief; they will reject the Holy One of Israel. Then the punishments of God will come upon them. He will send other nations to this land and he will give them power to take the land away from our people. There will be bloodshed for many years and our people [the Indians] will be beaten and scattered.

O my children, awake from your deep sleep and shake off the awful chains that keep you bound. Awake and arise from the dust. Hear the words of a trembling parent, whose limbs will soon lay down in the grave.

My heart has been weighed down with sorrow because of you. I fear that because of the hardness of your hearts, the Lord will curse your people for many generations with wars and hunger and leave you hated. The Lord has said: If you keep my commandments, you will grow in the land; but if do not keep my commandments, you will be cut off.

Do not fight against your brother Nephi. His views have been wonderful and he has kept the commandments. If not for him, we would have died of hunger in the wilderness or drowned in the sea. I fear and tremble that because of you, he will suffer again. You say he seeks power over you, but he does not. He seeks only the glory of God and your own eternal welfare.

You complain because Nephi spoke plainly. You say he used sharp words. His sharpness is the sharpness of God's word. You say he was angry with you. What you call anger is truth. God's power is with him.

2nd Nephi 2

The way to God is prepared and salvation is free. Everything has opposites so people can choose light or dark, good or bad, spiritual life or spiritual death, righteousness or sin. With righteousness, there is happiness. With sin, there is sadness.

All people are taught enough to know good from evil. Still, all people sin. So Jesus will pay the price for sin so all people who have a repentant heart and a humble spirit can be forgiven.

No one can live with God without the mercy and grace of Jesus, the Holy Messiah. He will lay down his life and lift it up again by the power of the Spirit. He will give the gift of resurrection to all people.

The Lord has saved my soul. I have seen his glory and I am surrounded in the arms of his love. My sons, look to Jesus and choose eternal life. Amen.

2nd Nephi 3

Now I, Lehi, speak to Joseph, my last child. You were born in the wilderness. You are a descendant of Joseph who was carried captive into Egypt. He truly saw our day.

The Lord said to Joseph: I will raise up another prophet to

bring my word to your people. His name will be Joseph [Joseph Smith, Junior] and his father also will be named Joseph [Joseph Smith, Senior].

Blessed are you, my son. You are little, so listen to your brother, Nephi, and remember the words of your dying father. Amen.

2nd Nephi 4

Then my father brought together the children of Laman and blessed them. Then he brought to him the children of Lemuel and he blessed them. Then he blessed the sons of Ishmael and all their families. Then he blessed Sam. Then my father, Lehi, died and we buried his body.

I, Nephi, trust God. He led me through hardships in the desert. He rescued me on the waters of the great deep ocean. He filled me with his love. He caused my enemies to shake before me. He heard my prayers by day. He gave me visions at night.

I have become bold in mighty prayer to God. I have sent my voice up high and angels have come down and blessed me. His Spirit has carried me away to high mountains. My eyes have seen great things that are too great for man to see or hear.

So, if I have seen so great things, if the Lord in his love has visited men in so much mercy, why does my heart weep? Why does my soul stay in the valley of sorrow and my strength weaken because of my problems?

Why should I give in to sin? Why should I give in to temptations that the evil one has placed in my heart to hurt my soul? Why am I angry because of my enemy?

My heart cries: O pitiful man that I am! My heart is sad because of my sins. I am surrounded by temptations that easily trap me. When I want to be happy, my heart groans because of my sin.

Awake, my soul! Droop no more in sin. Be happy my heart. Do not anger because of your enemies. Do not lose strength because of your problems.

Be happy my heart. Pray to the Lord. Say to him: O Lord, I will praise you forever. My soul will have joy in you, the rock of my salvation. O Lord, make me shake at the first sign of sin. O Lord, make a way for me to escape my enemies! Clear the way before me. O Lord, I have trusted in you and I will trust in you forever.

2nd Nephi 5

I, Nephi, prayed much for my brothers, but their anger increased against me. They tried to kill me. They complained: Our younger brother wants to rule us. The right to rule belongs to us, the older brothers. We will kill him and have no more trouble with him.

The Lord warned me to go into the wilderness and take all who would go with me. I took with me my family, Zoram and his family, Sam, my older brother and his family, Jacob and Joseph, my younger brothers, and my sisters. Those who went with me were those who believed the words of God.

We took our tents and everything we could carry. After traveling for many days, we pitched our tents. My people called the place Nephi. All those who were with me called themselves the people of Nephi.

We were careful to obey all God's commandments. The Lord was with us and we were greatly blessed. We had good farms and flocks and animals of every kind.

We built buildings and worked with wood, iron, copper, brass, steel, gold and silver which were plentiful.

I, Nephi, built a temple. It was like the temple of Solomon. Thirty years had passed from the time we left Jerusalem. We lived in the manner of happiness.

With the sword of Laban as a model, I made many swords to protect us from the people of Laman. The Lamanites' hatred toward us was strong. God caused a curse to come on them because of their sins. God turned their skin dark.

The Lord said: If your brothers will not listen to your words they will be cut off from me.

2nd Nephi 6 to 8

[These chapters contain writings that are written by the prophet Isaiah. They were written in the brass plates and in the Bible.]

2nd Nephi 9

Because of the blessings of the Lord, I hope you will find happiness and lift up your head forever. The great Creator [Jesus Christ] will come to earth and overcome death for all people. As death must come to all people, a power to overcome death must also come.

O the wisdom of God, his mercy and grace! For if the body could live no more, our spirits would be shut out from the presence of God. The Lord will bring resurrection to everyone. The spirit and the body will be restored to itself again to live forever and die no more.

All people must appear before the judgment-seat of Jesus to be judged by God's holy judgment. Those who are clean will stay clean. Those who are filthy will stay filthy. Good people will have a perfect knowledge of their goodness. Bad people will have a knowledge of all their shame.

The righteous saints who believed in the Holy One of Israel and stayed good through all the tests of the world will be given the kingdom of God. Their joy will be full forever.

Jesus Christ will come into the world so that all can be saved. He will suffer the pains of all people, yes, the pains of all men, women and children.

He commands all people to repent and be baptized in his name. We must have perfect faith in Jesus Christ to be saved in the kingdom of God.

O the foolishness of men! When they are educated, they

think they are wise. They do not listen to the words of God. They put it aside and think they know better by themselves. Their wisdom is foolishness and it will not help them. They will be destroyed. To be educated is good only if you obey God's words.

Trouble comes to the rich if the rich hate the poor and hurt the meek, and if their hearts are on their treasures. Their treasure becomes their God, so both they and their treasure will perish.

Trouble comes to the liar; he will be thrust down to hell. Trouble comes to the murderer who deliberately kills; he will die. Remember the awfulness of sinning against God. Focusing on worldly things leads to death. Focusing on spiritual things leads to eternal life.

Do not say I have spoken hard things against you. I have spoken the words of your Maker. I know the words of truth are hard against sinners. Good people do not fear; they love the truth.

God hates people who are proud of being wise, educated, or rich. God will save them only when they throw these things away, come to him in deep humility and see themselves as fools before him.

Come everyone who thirsts. If you have no money, come buy drink without money. Do not spend money for that which is of no worth. Do not do work for things that cannot satisfy.

Remember God's words. Pray to him always by day. Give thanks to his holy name by night. Be happy.

2nd Nephi 10

Now I, Jacob, speak to you about Jesus Christ who is to come. Last night the angel told me Jesus would come to the Jews. The Jews are a wicked people. They will kill Jesus. No other nation on earth would crucify their God.

If such mighty miracles were done among other nations, the people would repent and know Jesus is their God. But because of priests who want money and power, the Jews at Jerusalem will stiffen their necks and kill Jesus.

For this, God will send destruction, hunger and bloodshed. He will scatter the Jews among all nations. But the Lord God said: When the day comes that the Jews believe in me, that I am Christ, I will then give their lands [Israel] back to them.

God said this land [Americas] will be a land for your people [the Indians]. This land will be a land of freedom for the Gentiles and there will be no kings on the land. I will make this land strong against all other nations.

The Lord's promises are great even to the people who are on the islands of the sea. From time to time, the Lord has led away the people of Israel and scattered them around the world. Just as he remembers us, the Lord will remember all his people.

Cheer up your hearts. Remember you are free to act for yourselves to choose the way of eternal life.

2nd Nephi 11

My soul delights in proving to my people the truth of the coming of Christ. My soul delights in proving to my people that Christ can save all people.

2nd Nephi 12 through 24

[Writings by the prophet Isaiah. They are also written in the brass plates and in the Bible.]

2nd Nephi 25

Six hundred years after my father left Jerusalem, the Son of God will live on the earth. The Jews will reject him and crucify Him. After his body lays in a tomb for three days, he will rise from the dead. Then Jesus will show himself to people who believe in him. All who believe will be saved in the kingdom of

God.

Jerusalem will again be destroyed. Awful punishments come to anyone who fights against God and the people of his church. The Jews will be scattered among all nations. God will punish them by other nations for many years until the Jews believe in Jesus.

The day will come when the Jews will believe Jesus Christ is God's Son, the great Messiah, the Holy Redeemer and Savior of all people. They will worship the Father in the name of Christ with pure hearts and clean hands.

There is no other person except Jesus Christ who can save you. We work hard to help our children and families to believe in Christ. For after people do all they can do, they are saved only by the mercy of God.

We talk of Christ. We are happy in Christ. We preach of Christ. We prophesy of Christ so our children may know where to look for forgiveness of their sins.

My people in the last days [Indians] will be stubborn. I speak plainly so you must understand. These words are enough to teach anyone the right way.

The right way is to believe in Christ and not reject him. Christ is the Holy One of Israel. You must bow down to God and worship him with all your might, mind and strength and your whole soul. If you do this, you will be given eternal life.

2nd Nephi 26

After Christ rises from the dead, he will show himself [in the Americas] to our people. Signs will be given at his birth, death and resurrection. Christ's death will be terrible to the wicked, for they will die.

The good people who listen to the prophets' words and look forward to the signs of Christ will not die. God's Son will show himself to them, he will heal them and they will have peace for three generations.

But in the fourth generation, a speedy destruction will

come to my people. I have seen it in a vision. Their pride and foolishness will bring them death. The Lord's Spirit does not stay with evil people. When the Spirit leaves, destruction soon follows.

After the people of Nephi and the people of Laman shrink in unbelief, they will be beaten by the Gentiles [Europeans]. The Lord will send Gentiles to camp against them and attack them with horses. The Gentiles will build forts against them and bring the Lamanites [the Indians] down low in the dust.

But the Gentiles will lift themselves up in their own pride. The Gentiles will stumble, because they build up churches that ignore the power and miracles of God. They will preach their own ideas to get money. These churches will cause jealousy and fighting and hate. There will be secret groups led by the devil.

The Lord does not work in darkness. Everything He does is for the blessing of His children. He loves us so much He will lay down his own life to bring us to Him.

He invites all to come. He does not say to some: Leave me. No, he says: All of you come to Me. Buy milk and honey without money and without price. He gives salvation free to all. He commands everyone to repent. To God, all people are alike.

The Lord says all people must have charity, which is love. If they have no charity, they are nothing. He commands us to not murder, lie, steal, swear the name of God, envy, hate and fight. Anyone who does these things will be punished.

No sin comes from the Lord. He does good things for people. He invites all to come to him, black and white, slave and free, male and female. All are alike to God.

2nd Nephi 27

In the last days, both those who will come on this land [Americas] and those who will be on other lands will be drunken in sin. When that day comes, they will be visited by the Lord with thunder and earthquakes and storms and the flame of swallowing fire.

All nations who fight against Zion will be like a hungry man who eats in his dreams but wakes up and finds his soul is empty.

God will bring you the words of a book [Book of Mormon]. They will be the words of a people who have slept. The words of this book will be read on the housetops and they will be read by the power of Christ.

The gold plates will be hidden from the eyes of the world. No one will see them except three witnesses. They will testify of the truth of the book. No others will see the book except a few by the will of God. They, too, will testify of God's word.

God will bring part of the book to the world. Then it will be sealed up again and hidden up to God until the people are ready for more. Many people say they love God and with their lips, they honor him, but their hearts are far from him. Their fear of God is created by the men's ideas.

2nd Nephi 28

The things written in the book will be of great worth to all people and especially to our people [the Indians]. In the last days there will be many churches, but not to the Lord.

Some will say: I am the Lord's church. Others will say: I am the Lord's church. They will argue with each other. Their priests will argue with each other. They will teach their own learning and reject the Holy Ghost.

There will be many who say: Eat, drink and be merry, for tomorrow we die and it will turn out fine. There will be many who say: Eat, drink and be merry, but fear God.

They say: God will allow a little sin. Lie a little; take advantage of others because of their words; dig a pit for your neighbor to fall in. There is no harm in this. Do all these things, for tomorrow we die. If we are guilty, God will beat us with a few stripes, but in the end he will bring us in his kingdom.

Many people will teach such false and foolish ideas. Many will puff up and try to hide their thoughts from God.

Their churches will be rotten. They will rob the poor to get fancy churches. They will rob the poor to buy fancy clothes. They hurt the meek and the poor in heart, because they puff up in pride. They wear stiff necks and high heads.

They have all gone wrong except a few humble followers of Christ. Even those are led, in many cases, to do wrong because they are taught wrong ideas.

Trouble will come to all who treat the things of God like trash! The day will come when God will speedily visit the people of the earth. When they are fully ripe in sin, they will die. But if they repent, they will live.

The kingdom of the devil will shake. Those who belong to it must be stirred up to repent, or the devil will tie them with his chains and pull them down. In the last days, Satan will fill the hearts of many people and make them hate good things.

Satan will trick many by telling them that there is no hell. He tricks others by giving them false comfort. He wants them to think that everything is fine, so they will say: All is well in Zion. All is well. In this way, the devil cheats their souls and leads them carefully down to hell.

Trouble will come to those who are sleepy in Zion! And to those who say: All is well! Those who listen to the ideas of men and put aside the power of God and the gift of the Holy Ghost must beware!

Trouble will come to all who say: We have enough and we need no more! Trouble will come to all who say: We have the word of God and we need no more!

God says: I will give people knowledge line on line, idea on idea, here a little and there a little. Blessed are those who listen to My teachings for they will learn wisdom. Those who accept My word will be given more. Those who say they have enough will lose what they have.

2nd Nephi 29

In the last days, many of the Gentiles will say: A Bible! A Bible! We have a Bible and there cannot be any more Bible.

God says: O fools, you accept the Bible without thanking the Jews. Do they remember the hardships and pains of the Jews and their hard work in bringing salvation to the Gentiles? No. You have cursed the Jews and have hated them and have not tried to help them. But I, the Lord, have not forgotten my people.

Those fools who say: A Bible, we have a Bible and we need no more Bible. You should know there are more nations than one. You should know that I, the Lord God, have created all people. I remember those on the islands of the sea and I bring My word to all nations.

Why do you complain when you get more of My word? Do you know that the testimony of two nations is a witness to you that I am God. I remember one nation like another and I speak the same words to all nations. When two nations come together, My words to both nations come together also.

I do this to prove I am the same yesterday, today and forever. Just because I have spoken one word, do not think I cannot speak another. My work is never finished.

Just because you have a Bible, you should not think you have all my words. I command all people in the east, in the west, in the north and in the south and in the islands of the sea to write the words I speak. I will judge all people out of these books.

I speak to the Jews and they write it. I also speak to the Nephites and they write it. I speak to the other tribes of the people of Israel and they write it. I speak to all nations of the earth and they write it.

In the last days, the Jews will have the words of the Nephites [Book of Mormon]. The Nephites will have the words of the Jews [Bible]. The Nephites and the Jews will have the words of the lost tribes of Israel. The lost tribes of Israel will have the words of the Nephites and Jews.

Just as My people of Israel will be gathered home, so will

My words be gathered together in one. I will show those who fight against My word and against My people that I am God. I will finish the promise I made to Abraham to remember his people forever.

2nd Nephi 31

I, Nephi, speak to you plainly. The Lord works in plainness among the children of men. For the Lord speaks to them by their language and their understanding.

God sets the example for us and shows us the straightness of the path and the narrowness of the gate by which we must enter. He says: Follow Me. I ask: How can we follow Jesus unless we are willing to keep the commandments of the Father?

The Father said: Repent, repent and be baptized in the name of my Beloved Son. And the voice of the Son came to me, saying: He that is baptized in My name, the Father will give the Holy Ghost. So, follow Me and do the things which you have seen Me do.

Follow the Son with full purpose of heart. Act sincerely with no deception. Repent of your sins. Witness to the Father that you are willing to take on you the name of Christ, by baptism, then you will receive the Holy Ghost.

The gate by which you must enter is repentance and baptism by water. Then comes forgiveness by the Holy Ghost. Then you are in the strait and narrow path which leads to eternal life.

After you are on the strait and narrow path, I ask: Is all done? No. You must move on with faith in Christ, have hope and a love of God and of all men. You must press forward, feast on the words of Christ and endure to the end. Then you will have eternal life.

I heard a voice from the Father, saying: All who continue to the end will be saved. This is the way; and there is no other way or name under heaven to save you in the kingdom of God.

2nd Nephi 32

The Holy Ghost will show you all things you should do. The Spirit teaches people to pray. The devil teaches people to not pray. I say you must pray always and not faint. You should not do anything for the Lord until you pray to the Father in the name of Christ for him to bless your work.

2nd Nephi 33

I, Nephi, cannot write all the things taught to my people. I am not mighty in writing, like I am in speaking. When a man speaks by the Holy Ghost, the power of the Holy Ghost carries it to your heart.

The words I write are of great worth, especially to my people. I pray for them by day. My eyes water my pillow for them at night, that the words I have written in weakness will be made strong to them and help them do good, to believe in Jesus and to hang on to the end.

My brothers and Jews and all the people of the earth, listen to these words and believe in Christ. If you believe in Christ, you will believe these words. They are Christ's words, for He has given them to me. They teach all people to do right.

If you judge these are not his words, Christ will show you at the last day with power and great glory that they are His. I pray to the Father in the name of Christ that many of us, if not all, will be saved in His kingdom.

I speak to you like a voice from the dust. I say farewell to you until that great day.

JACOB
Brother of Nephi

Jacob 1

Fifty-five years have passed since we left Jerusalem. We work hard to help our people come to Christ and enjoy God's goodness.

Nephi was growing old. He told me, Jacob, to take care of the records. He chose a man to rule in his place; then Nephi died. He had served the people all his life and the people loved him greatly. The people wanted to honor him. They decided new rulers would be named after him, second Nephi, third Nephi and so on.

There were many people on the land: Nephites, Jacobites, Josephites, Ishmalites, Zoramites, Lamanites and Lemuelites. All who were friendly to Nephi were called Nephites. Those who tried to destroy the Nephites were called Lamanites.

The Nephites began to search for gold and silver and to be full of pride.

Jacob 2

Jacob, the brother of Nephi, spoke to the Nephites. He said: I come to the temple to tell you God's word. With the help of the all-powerful God, I tell you your thoughts.

You are beginning to try sin. I am sad that I must say these things about you in front of your wives and children, whose feelings are tender.

Many of you search for gold and silver, which is plentiful in this land. It is true that the hand of God has smiled on you with many riches. But some of you lift yourselves in pride. You have stiff necks and high heads because of the cost of your clothes. You put down others because you think you are better than they.

Do you think that God will help you do this? I say to you, no. He will punish you. He could turn you to dust with one look of His eye! Do not let the pride of your hearts destroy your souls! Get rid of this sin.

Think of others as you think of yourselves. Be friendly with all and share your things, so others may be rich like you.

Before you seek for riches, seek for the kingdom of God. After you have a hope in Christ, you can seek for riches if you want. Use it to help others—to get clothes for the poor and food for the hungry and freedom for the slaves and help for the sick.

You have done worse sins than pride. You have not been true to your wives; you have broken their hearts. You have lost the confidence of your children because of your bad example. The Lord says: I delight in chastity. I hear the cries of my fair daughters against their husbands.

Jacob 3

The Lamanites are better than you. Lamanite husbands love their wives. Their wives love their husbands. Lamanite husbands and their wives love their children.

Think of your children. Your bad example may bring them to destruction. Their sins will be put on your heads.

Shake yourselves; wake up your good sense. Rise from the sleep of death. You who are pure in heart, lift your heads and accept God's pleasing word. Feast on his love.

Jacob 4

I, Jacob, can write only a few of my words, because of the difficulty of writing words onto these metal plates. But if we write on anything else, it will wear off in time. So we work hard to engrave these words on plates, hoping you will read them with thankful hearts.

We have written these things to show we knew of Christ many hundreds of years before he came to earth. We have many visions and prophecies. With all this proof, our faith is strong. In the name of Jesus, we can command the trees, or mountains, or waves of the sea to obey us.

God shows us our weakness. We know it is by his mercy and love that we are given power to do these things. By God's power, the world was created. By his word, people came on the earth. It is impossible for people to find out all his ways. The only way to know God is when he sends revelations by the Holy Ghost.

Jacob 5-6

I beg you, repent and cling to God as he clings to you. His arm of mercy reaches toward you. Do not harden your hearts. Enter in at the strait gate and stay in the narrow way until you have eternal life. Be wise; what more can I say?

Jacob 7

After some years, a man named Sherem came to the Nephites. He began to preach that there would be no Christ. He said many flattering words to the people. He worked hard and led away many people.

He wanted to speak to me, because I, Jacob, believed in Christ. He was educated and spoke clever, tricky words. He tried to shake me away from my faith. But I have seen angels and they have blessed me. I have heard the voice of the Lord speaking to me. So I could not be shaken.

Sherem said to me: Brother Jacob, I have heard that you go preaching the gospel of Christ. You have led away many of these people to worship a person that you say will come many hundreds of years from now. I, Sherem, say to you that no man can know such things, for no one can tell of things to come.

In this way, Sherem argued against me. But the Lord God put his Spirit in my soul. I said to Sherem: Do you deny that Christ will come? He answered: If there would be a Christ, I would not deny him. But I know that there is no Christ, neither has been, nor ever will be.

Sherem said: Show me a sign, if you know so much. I said to him: I would not tempt God to show you a sign about something that you already know to be true. You would still reject it, because you are of the devil. But God will strike you down. Let that be a sign to you that Christ will come and that God has all power.

When I, Jacob, said these words, the power of the Lord came on Sherem, so he fell to the earth. The people watched over him for several days. One day Sherem awoke and said to the people: Gather together tomorrow, for I will die. When the people were gathered, he spoke to them.

He told of the truth of Christ and the power of the Holy Ghost. He told the people that he had been tricked by the devil. After he said these words, he could say no more and he died. The people were amazed. The power of God came down on them. This was pleasing to me, for I had asked Heavenly Father to do this. Now peace and the love of God came again to the people.

We tried many ways to bring the Lamanites to know of the truth. It was useless. They enjoyed wars and bloodshed. They hated us and they tried to kill us all the time. So we Nephites made our cities strong. We trusted in God.

Our lives passed like a dream. We were a lonesome people. We were wanderers born in a wilderness and hated by our brothers. With many wars and fighting, we suffered out our lives.

I, Jacob, saw that I would soon go down to my grave. I said to my son Enos: Take these plates. I say to you: Farewell.

ENOS
Son of Jacob

I am Enos. My father taught me the ways of the Lord and I thank God for it.

I will tell you about the wrestle I had before God because of my sins. I went to hunt food in the forests, but it was my soul that was hungry. The words I often heard my father speak about eternal life and the joy of the saints sank deep in my heart.

I kneeled down and cried to God in mighty prayer for my soul. I prayed to him all day long. When the night came, I still cried my voice high to the heavens. At last, a voice said to me: Enos, your sins are forgiven and you will be blessed.

All my guilt and shame was swept away. I asked: Lord, how is this done? He said to me: Your faith in Christ whom you have neither heard nor seen has made you whole.

When I heard these words, I began to care for my brothers, the Nephites. I poured out my whole soul to God for them. While I was praying, the voice of the Lord came to my mind again, saying: I will visit your brothers. I have given them this land and it is a Holy Land, but their sins will bring sadness on their own heads.

After I heard these words, my faith in God began to be strong. I also prayed long hours for my brothers, the Lamanites. They had promised in anger they would kill us and destroy our books.

I knew the Lord God would be able to save our books. He said to me: Whatever you ask in faith in the name of Christ, you will have. God promised me He would save our books and bring them to the Lamanites in His own time.

I went among the Nephites, teaching them the things to

come. My people tried to bring the Lamanites to true faith in God, but their hatred was strong. They were wild, cruel and bloodthirsty.

They ate lions and tigers. They lived in tents and wandered in the wilderness with a short skin around their waists. Their heads were shaved. Many of them ate only raw meat. Their skill was the bow and arrow and war ax. They always tried to kill us.

The Nephites farmed grains and fruits and raised herds of cattle, goats and horses. There were many prophets among us. But our people were also a stubborn people. The only thing that kept them in fear of the Lord was harsh preaching of wars and death and the length of eternity and God's judgments and power.

One hundred and seventy nine years had passed from the time that Lehi left Jerusalem. I saw many wars between the Nephites and Lamanites in my life.

I saw I would soon die. I looked forward to the day when I would stand before my Savior. I will see His face with pleasure and He will say to me: Come to Me, there is a place prepared for you in the kingdom of My Father. Amen.

JAROM

I, Jarom, am the son of Enos. My father told me to write a few words about the people. Many among us have visions. We are not all stubborn. Those who have faith are blessed with the Holy Spirit.

In the two hundredth year, the Nephites were strong in the land. They kept the Law of Moses and kept the Sabbath Day holy. They did not swear.

We became rich in gold, silver, fine wood, buildings, machinery, iron, copper, brass and steel. We made all kinds of tools to farm the ground. We made all kinds of weapons, sharp pointed arrows, the dart and the javelin to defend ourselves from the Lamanites.

The prophets, priests and teachers worked hard to help the people repent, look to the Lord, and believe in Him as if He had already come.

OMNI

My father, Jarom, told me, Omni, to write on these plates. In my days, I fought much with the sword to save my people from the Lamanites. We had many seasons of peace and we had many seasons of terrible war. But I am a wicked man and I have not kept the commandments of the Lord as I should have. I give the plates to my son Amaron.

I, Amaron, write in the three hundred twentieth year. The Lamanites killed the most evil part of the Nephites. The Lord protected the good people. I give the plates to my brother Chemish.

I, Chemish, saw what Amaron wrote. He wrote it the day he gave the plates to me. In this way, we keep the records. It is the commandment of our fathers. Now I end.

I, Abinadom, am the son of Chemish. I saw much war. With my own sword, I have killed many of the Lamanites in the defense of my people.

I am Amaleki, the son of Abinadom. I speak to you about Mosiah, who was made king over the land of Zarahemla. He was warned by the Lord to flee the land of Nephi-Lehi. Those who listened to the voice of the Lord went with him to the wilderness.

They were led by the power of God to a land that is called Zarahemla. Mosiah discovered an unknown people living there, but he could not understand their language. Mosiah taught them his language.

These people had left Jerusalem when Zedekiah, king of Judah, was carried away prisoner to Babylon. The Lord also brought them across the sea to this land.

The people of Zarahemla had no books of their history. They were full of joy when they saw that Mosiah had the plates of brass that told the stories of the Jews. The people of Zarahemla and of Mosiah joined together. Mosiah was appointed to be their king.

One day, a large stone with engravings was brought to Mosiah and he explained the engravings by the gift and power of God. The stone also told a few words about their fathers who came out from the tower of Babel.

I, Amaleki, was born in the days of Mosiah. When he died, my brother Benjamin ruled in his place. Some of the people of Mosiah wanted to go back to the land of their birth, so they went to the land of Lehi-Nephi.

Their leader was a strong and stubborn man. He started a great argument among them and they were all killed, except fifty. Those who survived returned to Zarahemla. Zeniff took another group into the wilderness toward the land of Nephi. I had a brother who went with them. We have not heard from any of them since.

I began to be old. Because King Benjamin is a fair man, I gave him these plates. I wish you would come to Christ, the Holy One of Israel, and be saved. Come to Him and offer your whole soul to Him. Continue fasting and praying. Hang on to the end. Then you will be saved.

Mosiah
Son of Benjamin

Mosiah 1

The Lamanite armies came from the land of Nephi-Lehi to the land of Zarahemla to battle against us. King Benjamin gathered his armies. He fought with the sword of Laban. With the strength of the Lord, they killed many thousands of Lamanites and pushed them out.

King Benjamin had three sons: Mosiah, Helorum and Helaman. They were taught well. King Benjamin said to his sons: Without these plates, we would not know the words of God and we would suffer in ignorance.

My sons, if we did not have the words of God always before our eyes, we would shrink in unbelief and become like the Lamanites, who know nothing about these things. O my sons, these scriptures are true. Remember to search them well. Keep the commandments of God.

King Benjamin grew old. He brought Mosiah before him and said to him: My son, tell the people to gather together. Tomorrow I will tell them that you are their new king. Mosiah told the people to go to the temple to hear the words of his father.

Mosiah 2

When the people came to the temple, they pitched their tents round about, every family in its own area. But there were so many people that King Benjamin could not teach them all. His words were written and sent to those who could not hear.

He said: Open your hearts and minds so you will understand the mysteries of God. Do not fear me or think that I am more than a mortal man. I am like you. I have weaknesses in body and mind. I was chosen by you and allowed by the Lord to be your ruler king. I have served you with all the strength that the Lord has given me.

I did not take gold or silver or riches from you. I have not allowed you to be put in prisons, or allowed anyone to be a slave. I have worked with my own hands to serve you, so that you would not be loaded down with taxes. I have spent all my days in your service. I do not boast, for I have only been serving God. When you serve people, you are serving God.

If I, your earthly king, deserve any thanks from you, how much more you should thank your Heavenly King! I say to you, give all the thanks and praise of your whole soul to God. Serve God who has created you and keeps you alive from day to day.

God gives you breath and helps you from one moment to the next. All He asks is that you keep His commandments. Always give God thanks. He gives you far more than you can give in return. Give to Him all that you have and are.

Think of the blessings and happiness of those who keep God's commandments. Think of the awful life of those who sin.

I can no longer be your teacher or king. The Lord told me to tell you that my son Mosiah will now be your king and ruler.

Mosiah 3

An angel said to me: Awake, I come to tell you words of great joy. The Lord has heard your prayers. Soon the Lord will come down from heaven and live on the earth as a man. He will go among people working mighty miracles, healing the sick and raising the dead. He will cause the crippled to walk, the blind to see and the deaf to hear.

He will suffer temptations, pain, hunger, thirst and great tiredness even more than any person can suffer. To pay for the sins of the world, His pain will be so great that blood will come from every pore. He will be called Jesus Christ, Son of God, Father of heaven and earth, Creator of all things. His mother will be called Mary.

After all He will do, evil people will whip Him and kill Him. But He will rise from the dead in three days.

He will forgive the sins of those who died without knowing the word of God. But He will not forgive those who keep sinning when they know the gospel, unless they repent and have faith in the Lord Jesus Christ.

The Lord God sends his holy prophets to every people. They teach that all who believe in Christ will have forgiveness and great joy.

The Lord saw that His people would be a stubborn people. So He will give many signs about His coming. All people must become like little children: meek, humble, patient, full of love, willing to submit to all things that the Lord sees fit to put on them.

Mosiah 4

After King Benjamin finished speaking, he saw that the crowd had fallen to the ground. The fear of God came over them. They all cried with one voice: Have mercy. Forgive our sins. We believe in Jesus Christ, the Son of God.

Then the Spirit of the Lord came on them and filled them with joy. King Benjamin said to them: Salvation comes to those who trust the Lord. Obey His words and hang on to the end of this life. Believe in God, believe that He is and that He created all things. Believe that He has all wisdom and all power, both in heaven and in earth. Man does not understand all that the Lord understands.

If you believe all these things, do them. If you do them, you will always be happy and be filled with the love of God. You will grow in the knowledge of God and in the knowledge of that which is just and true.

You will not want to hurt each other. You will want peace.

You will not allow your children to go hungry. You will not allow them to fight and quarrel with each other. Teach them to walk in the ways of truth. Teach them to love each other and serve each other.

You will help those who need your help. You will share your things with those who are in need. You will not allow the beggar to go away empty or turn him out to die. Do not say: This person has caused his own misery, so I will not give him food.

Whoever does this has great reason to repent. Unless he repents, he will have no place in the kingdom of God. We are all beggars. We all depend on God for all we have.

You have been praying and begging for forgiveness of your sins. He has not allowed you to beg in vain. He has poured out His Spirit on you and filled your hearts with joy. Your joy was so great you could not speak.

God gives you what you need, so you should give to each other. Do all in wisdom and order. You are not asked to do more than you have strength to do. Be steady so you will win the prize.

Watch yourselves; watch your thoughts and words and deeds. Keep God's commandments. Hang on to the end of your life and you will be happier. Remember and be happy.

Mosiah 5

Then the people all cried with one voice, saying: We believe all the words that you said. The Lord's Spirit has made a mighty change in our hearts. We have no more desire to do evil, but to do good always. Our joy is so great.

We promise with God to do His wishes and obey Him all the days of our lives. Then King Benjamin said to them: Because of the promise that you have made, you will be called the children of Christ, His sons and daughters.

Take on you the name of Christ. Always keep His name written in your hearts. Know the voice that will one day call you. People only know the master they serve and keep near to their thoughts and heart. Always do good works so the Lord may call you His and give you eternal life.

Mosiah 6

Mosiah began to rule. King Benjamin lived three more years. King Mosiah and his people farmed the earth. There was no arguing for three years.

Mosiah 7

King Mosiah wanted to know about the people who went to live in the land of Lehi-Nephi. Nothing had been heard from them since they left.

King Mosiah sent sixteen strong men to go to the land of Lehi-Nephi to find out about their brothers. Ammon was their leader. They wandered for forty days in the wilderness until they found the land of Nephi.

Ammon took Amaleki, Helem and Hem and went to meet their king, but the king had his guards surround them, tie them and put them in prison. After two days, they were taken to the king and their ropes were loosed. They stood before the king to answer his questions.

He said to them: I am Limhi, the son of Noah and grandson of Zeniff, who came out of the land of Zarahemla. I want to know why you were so bold as to come near the walls of the city when I was out there with my guards?

Ammon bowed himself before the king and said: O king, I am thankful to God that I am still alive and am permitted to speak. I am sure that if you had known me, you would not have allowed me to be tied up. For I am Ammon and I have come out of the land of Zarahemla to ask about our brothers, whom Zeniff led.

When Limhi heard these words, he was glad. He said: Now I know that my brothers in the land of Zarahemla are still alive. For we are slaves to the Lamanites. They tax us heavily. Maybe our brothers in Zarahemla will rescue us from the Lamanites. If they do, we will be their slaves. For it is better to be slaves to the Nephites than pay taxes to the Lamanites.

King Limhi told his guards to untie Ammon and his brothers. The king sent the guards to bring the rest of Ammon's group to the city to eat, drink and rest. They were suffering hunger, thirst and weariness.

King Limhi gathered his people to hear him speak. King Limhi said: My people, lift up your heads. The time is not far away when we will no longer be slaves to our enemies. Lift your heads and be happy. Put your trust in God, who brought the children of Israel out of Egypt through the Red Sea on dry ground.

It is because of our sins that he has let us walk into trouble. You all are witnesses this day that Zeniff was too eager to live in the land of Nephi-Lehi. He let us get tricked by evil King Laman. They make us pay hard taxes.

Today we pay to the king of the Lamanites half our corn and all our grains and half the increase of our flocks and our herds and half of all we have to the king of the Lamanites. This is too much to take away from our lives. It is great reason to feel sad.

Do not wonder why we are punished with terrible sufferings. The Lord has said: I will not support my people in their sins. I will block their ways so they will not grow. Their efforts will make them stumble.

And God says: if my people will plant sin, they will harvest poison. So the promise of the Lord came true and we are punished and hurt. But if we will turn to the Lord with full purpose of heart, put our trust in Him and serve Him with all our minds, He will rescue us from slavery.

Mosiah 8

Then Ammon stood before the crowd and told all that had happened in Zarahemla from the time Zeniff left the land.

Ammon told them the words of King Benjamin and the words from the brass plates.

Later, King Limhi asked Ammon if he could understand strange languages. Ammon told him that he could not. The king said to him: Some time ago, I sent forty-three men into the wilderness toward the land of Zarahemla. I had hoped that we might find your people to help us out of our slavery. But they were lost in the wilderness for many days and could not find Zarahemla. They returned to this land having traveled in a land among many waters.

They discovered a land that was covered with bones of men and beasts. The land was covered with old buildings of every kind. It must have had many people.

My men brought back a large chest with rusty swords and shields made of brass and of copper. They also brought twenty-four plates made of pure gold which had many words written in them. [These plates tell of the people of Jared. You will read about them later in the Book of Ether.]

Ammon said to him: I can tell you, O king, of a man that can understand the words on the plates. He has a tool from God that helps him to understand all records; it is a gift from God. This tool is called an interpreter and no man can look in them unless God tells him to. Whoever God tells to use it is called a seer.

A seer is greater than a prophet. This is the greatest gift a man can have on the earth. A seer can know of things in the past and also of things in the future. Thus, God has provided a way for man, through faith, to work mighty miracles. The seer who can understand this record is the king of Zarahemla; he has this high gift from God.

Then King Limhi was happy and gave thanks to God, saying: A great mystery is written on these plates. Wonderful are the works of the Lord; He suffers patiently with His people. For people do not seek wisdom. They do not want wisdom to rule over them! People are as a wild flock of sheep that run away from the shepherd and are scattered and driven and eaten by the beasts of the forest.

Mosiah 9

King Limhi told Ammon the story of those who left Zarahemla many years ago. This is the story: I, Zeniff, was taught in the language of the Nephites and I know of the land of Nephi, our fathers' first land. I was sent as a spy among the Lamanites that I might spy out their forces, so that our army might come on them and kill them. But I saw they were a good people. So, I argued with our ruler to make a treaty with them. But our ruler was a narrow minded and bloodthirsty man.

He said that I should be killed, but I was rescued. Father fought against father and brother against brother, until most of our men were killed in the wilderness. Those who were spared returned to Zarahemla, to tell our tale to their wives and their children.

I was eager to go back to the land of Nephi. All who wanted to go to our old land went into the wilderness. But we were punished with hunger, for we were slow to remember our God.

After many days wandering in the wilderness, we pitched our tents near the land of Nephi. I went again with four of my men into the city of Lamanites, to the king, so I might find out the mood of the king.

He promised me we could live in the land of Lehi-Nephi and the land of Shilom. He told his people to leave that land so my people could have it.

We rebuilt the buildings and walls of Lehi-Nephi and Shilom. We farmed the ground with corn, wheat, barley and all kinds of fruits. We began to prosper.

But the king's agreement was a trick to bring my people into bondage. The Lamanites were a lazy people. They wanted us to be their slaves so they could live by the work of our hands and feast on the flocks of our fields. After we had lived in the land for twelve years, King Laman began to stir up his people to fight with my people. There began to be wars and trouble in the land.

South of Shilom my people were farming and feeding their flocks. A great army of Lamanites attacked them. The army took their flocks and the corn of our fields. Those who were not killed ran into the city of Nephi.

I gave our people bows, arrows, swords, clubs and slings and all kinds of weapons we could invent. We went against the Lamanites. We prayed mightily to the Lord for Him to save us from our enemies.

God heard our prayers. He gave us power. In one day and one night we killed three thousand and forty three Lamanites. We pushed them out of our land. I helped bury their dead. To our great sadness, two hundred seventy nine of our brothers were killed.

Mosiah 10

We began to build the kingdom and we again had peace. Still, we made many weapons for my people in case the Lamanites would war against us. I set guards round the land so the Lamanites could not come in surprise.

Our men farmed the ground and raised grains and fruits of every kind. Our women made cloth of every kind. We had good clothes. We had peace for twenty-two years.

Then King Laman died and his son ruled. He stirred up his people in hatred against us. I sent my spies to discover their plans.

The Lamanite armies came to the north of Shilom. They were armed with bows and arrows, swords, stones and slings. Their heads were shaved and they wore only a leather cloth.

I hid our women and children in the wilderness. All the men, young and old, gathered to battle against the Lamanites. I placed them in rows according to their ages. Even I, in my old age, battled against the Lamanites. And we went in the strength of the Lord to battle.

The Lamanites knew nothing of the Lord and his power.

They could use only their own strength. They were strong. They were wild and cruel warriors. They were taught by their grandfathers, Laman and Lemuel, to hate us.

I told these things to my men. It convinced them to battle with all their might and put their trust in the Lord. We battled with them face to face and killed them with a great slaughter. We drove them out of our land again.

Then we returned with our families to our homes to tend our flocks and farm our grounds. I, Zeniff, being old, gave the kingdom to my son Noah. May the Lord bless my people. Amen.

Mosiah 11

Noah was wicked. He was not true to his wife. This is terrible in the eyes of the Lord. Noah made the people pay tax of one fifth of all they had. He did this to support his sins and the sins of his priests.

He fired the good priests and put bad ones in their place. They were lifted in pride and were lazy. They would not work; they took what they wanted from the people.

The people became wicked, too. The priests taught the people that husbands and wives did not need to be true to each other. King Noah built many fancy buildings with gold and silver and iron and brass and copper. He forced the people to build him a palace and a throne of gold and silver and many fancy things.

The walls of the temple were decorated with fine wood, copper and brass. Golden couches were made for the high priests to rest on while they spoke lies to the people. King Noah built a high tower. It was so high that he could stand on the top and see all the land of Shilom and all the land of Shemlon.

He spent the riches he got from the people and he chased women. He made wine and became a drunk.

God would punish them when their sins were full. The Lamanites began to come in small numbers. King Noah's armies drove them back at first. The people bragged that their fifty could

55

fight against thousands of Lamanites.

There was a man among them whose name was Abinadi. He went among the people saying: The Lord has seen your evil. If you do not repent, God will visit you in anger. He will give you to your enemies and you will be brought into slavery. Then you will cry to God for help, but He will be slow to hear you.

When Abinadi finished, the people were angry. They tried to kill him, but the Lord rescued him.

When King Noah heard Abinadi's words, he was angry. He said: Who is Abinadi to judge me and my people? Who is this Lord that will bring hardship on my people? Bring Abinadi here so I can kill him. He has said these things to stir up my people against each other. I want to kill him.

The eyes of the people were blinded and their ears were hardened against the words of Abinadi. They tried to find him, but they could not catch him.

Mosiah 12

Two years later, the Lord said to Abinadi: Go tell my people they have not repented. Stretch out your hand and tell them: The Lord says you will become slaves to your enemies. You will be driven and killed. The vultures of the air and the dogs and the wild beasts will eat your bodies. The life of King Noah will be like a robe in a hot furnace. Then he will know I am the Lord.

I, the Lord, will make this hard-hearted people howl all day long. They will be treated and driven like stupid donkeys. I will send hail on them to punish and kill them. I will send insects to bite them and eat their grain. I will do this because of their sins.

Abinadi said many things that the people did not want to hear. They tied him and took him to the king. They said: We have brought a man who has said evil things about your people. He says God will destroy us.

He also says that your life will be like a robe in a furnace of fire. He says you will be like a thorny weed trampled down by animals and blown away by the wind. He says all this will happen to you if you do not repent. And he pretends God has said it. O king, you have not sinned. We are strong. How can we be slaves? This man has lied about you. We give him to you to punish.

Then the king and his priests began to question Abinadi to trick him. But he answered them boldly and confused them in their words. Abinadi said to them: Are you really priests? You only pretend to teach this people. I say you are abusing the words of the Lord! If you understood them, you have not taught them.

Why do you put your hearts on riches? Why do you commit sins by being untrue to your wives? You know that I speak the truth and you should tremble before God. You will soon be punished for your sins.

Mosiah 13

When King Noah heard these words, he said to his priests: Take him away and kill him. He is crazy. But when they tried to take him, Abinadi said: Do not touch me or God will kill you. I still have more to tell you. God will not let you kill me yet. The people did not dare touch him, for the Spirit of the Lord was with him. His face shined with a great glow.

He spoke with power and authority from God. He said: You see you have no power to kill me. I know my words about your sins go deep into your hearts. Yes, my words fill you with wonder and anger. After I finish, you may kill me if you wish. But I warn you, whatever you do to me will happen to you and your people.

But for now you must sit and listen while I read God's commandments. Do not have any other Gods. Do not use the name of the Lord your God in vain. Remember the Sabbath Day and keep it holy. Do all your work in six days. On the seventh day, do not work. Honor your father and mother.

Do not kill. Do not steal. Do not lie about your neighbor. Do not want your neighbor's house. Do not want your neighbor's wife.

Mosiah 14

[This chapter talks of Isaiah's prophecies about the coming of Jesus Christ.]

Mosiah 15

Abinadi said: The Lord will come down to live on earth. He will save His people. After He does mighty miracles, He will be killed. But He is stronger than death.

He will pay for the sins of all who repent. The Son of God has power over death. He will bring all back to life. But you should fear and tremble, for the Lord will not save those who fight against Him, or know the commandments of God and will not obey them.

Mosiah 16

The time will come when every person will see God eye to eye and confess before Him that His judgments are just. The bad people will be put out. They will howl and cry because they did not listen to the Lord.

Each of us will stand before the bar of God to be judged for our works. If they are good, we will be rewarded with eternal life and happiness. If our works are evil, we will be sent to the devil.

You should tremble and repent of your sins and remember you can be saved only through Christ. Amen.

Mosiah 17

When Abinadi finished, the king told the priests to take him and put him to death. There was a young priest there whose name was Alma. He believed the words of Abinadi. He begged the king to not be angry with Abinadi and allow him to leave in peace. Then the king was even more angry. He had Alma thrown out and sent his servants to kill him. Alma ran and hid. While he was hiding, he wrote what Abinadi had said.

The king said: Abinadi, we have found a crime against you and you must die. You have said that God Himself should come down and put us to death. But if you will take back all your words, I will let you live.

Abinadi said: I will not take back my words for they are true. I have allowed myself to be captured so you can kill me. Then my words and my blood will stand against you.

King Noah was afraid of Abinadi and was about to release him. But the priests shouted against Abinadi and began to say: O king, this man has insulted you. The priests got the king mad again so he would have Abinadi killed.

They took Abinadi, tied him and burned his skin with hot fire. When the flames began to hurt him, Abinadi cried out to them: Just as you have done this to me, so will some of your people suffer death by fire. In the future, some of your people will believe in the Lord and you will burn them as you burn me. And you will have killed your own people.

Those of you who will not believe will be punished with all kinds of diseases. You will be punished on every hand and scattered like a wild flock runs from savage beasts. You will be hunted and you will suffer, as I suffer, the pains of death by fire. For God will destroy those who will not obey.

Then Abinadi said: O God, receive my soul. When Abinadi said these words, he died and sealed the truth of his words with his death.

Mosiah 18

Alma, who had run from the servants of King Noah, repented of his sins and secretly taught the people the words of Abinadi. He taught about the things to come and also about the resurrection of the dead and about Christ and his resurrection and ascent to heaven.

Alma taught all who would listen. He taught them

privately, so that the king would not find out. Many believed Alma's words. All those who believed him went to a place called Mormon. It was on the borders of the land that was sometimes overrun with wild beasts.

There was, in Mormon, a fountain of pure water. Alma hid there in the daytime from the searches of the king. Many people went there to hear Alma's words. One day there was a large group gathered at the waters of Mormon.

Alma said: I know you want to come to God and be called His people and help each other. You are willing to be sad with those who are sad and give comfort to those who need comfort. You are willing to stand as witnesses of God at all times and in all places, even until death, that you may be saved by God and be given eternal life.

If this is the desire of your hearts, you should be baptized. Promise to serve God. Obey his commandments. If you do, He will send his Spirit to you.

When the people heard these words, they clapped their hands for joy. They said: This is the wish of our hearts. Alma then took Helam into the water and said: O Lord, pour out your Spirit on your servant that he may do this work with holiness of heart.

When Alma said these words, the Spirit of the Lord was with him. Alma said: Helam, I baptize you, having authority from the Almighty God, as a testimony that you have made a promise to serve him your whole life. May the Spirit of the Lord be poured out on you and may he grant to you eternal life through Christ.

After Alma said these words, both Alma and Helam went under the water and they came out of the water in joy, being filled with the Spirit. Then Alma took another, went a second time into the water and baptized him like the first.

In this way, Alma baptized every one that went to the place of Mormon about two hundred and four souls. They were filled with the mercy of God. They were called the Church of Christ. All who were baptized by the power and authority of God were added to His church.

Alma was given authority from God to ordain priests—one priest for every fifty members. He told them to teach only the things that he had taught and those things that were spoken by the mouths of the holy prophets. He told them to preach only repentance and faith on the Lord.

He told them that there should be no fighting and to have their hearts knit together in unity and love towards each other. They became the children of God. He told them to keep the Sabbath Day holy and give thanks to the Lord, their God, every day in prayer. One day in each week was set apart for them to gather together to teach each other and worship God.

He also told the priests to work with their own hands. Priests should not live on the people's money. They do the Lord's work, not for money, but for the mercy of God. They became strong in the Spirit and knowledge of God.

Alma told the people of the church to share their wealth. Those who had more shared with those who had less. They obeyed God, sharing with one another both the things of life and the things of the spirit.

All this was done in the forest that was near the waters of Mormon. But the king discovered them and sent his servants to watch them.

The king said Alma was stirring the people to fight against him, so he sent his army to destroy them. Alma learned about the coming army. He took his people and went into the wilderness. There were about four hundred fifty people.

Mosiah 19

King Limhi's army could not find them. And there began to be a division among Limhi's people. One group began to say threats against the king. There was a man among them whose name was Gideon. He was a strong man and an enemy to the king.

Gideon drew his sword and promised in his anger that he would kill the king. Gideon and the king began to fight each other. When the king saw that he was about to be killed, he ran and climbed up on his tower.

Gideon chased him and was about to get on the tower to kill the king. But the king noticed that the army of the Lamanites was coming. The king cried out in fear, saying: Gideon, spare me, the Lamanites are on us and will destroy us all. The king was not worried about his people; he was thinking about saving his own life. Gideon let him live.

The king told the people to run away from the Lamanites. They all took their women and children and ran away into the wilderness. The Lamanites chased them and began to kill them.

The king told his men to leave their wives and children behind. Many of the men would not leave them, but chose to stay. The rest of the men left their wives and children and ran away.

The men who stayed asked their daughters to beg the Lamanites not to kill them. The Lamanites had mercy on them, because of the charm of the women. So the Lamanites took them prisoner and carried them back to the land of Nephi.

The Lamanites gave them land, with two conditions. First, they must give King Noah to them. Second, they must agree to pay half of all they had, half of their gold and silver as a tax to the king of the Lamanites every year.

Limhi, one of the king's sons, was taken prisoner. He was a good man. When Limhi promised his people would pay taxes, the Lamanite King promised not to kill them. The Lamanites put guards around the land to keep the people of Limhi from leaving.

Gideon sent men into the wilderness to search for the king and those that were with him. The men they found were mad at King Noah for making them leave their wives and children behind. They had killed Noah with fire. The men were going to kill the priests, too, but the priests ran away into the wilderness. So the words of Abinadi were already coming true.

Mosiah 20

The priests of King Noah were ashamed to return. When a small group of the daughters of the Lamanites gathered to sing and dance and make merry, the evil priests discovered them and secretly watched them. The priests carried away twenty-four of the Lamanite daughters.

When the Lamanites learned their daughters were missing, they were angry with the people of Limhi. The Lamanites thought Limhi's people took them. The king went with his army to destroy the people of Limhi.

From the tower, Limhi saw the Lamanite army coming. He quickly gathered his people together and waited in the fields and forests. When the Lamanites came, the people of Limhi began to attack them from their hiding places and began to kill them. The battle became awful.

The Lamanites were twice as many as the people of Limhi. But the men of Limhi fought for their lives and for their wives and for their children; therefore they fought like dragons. And the Lamanites were pushed out.

They found the king of the Lamanites among the wounded, but he was not yet dead. When his wounds were treated, he was brought to King Limhi. Limhi asked him: Why did you come to war against my people? My people have not broken the promise I made to you.

The Lamanite king said: I have broken my promise because your people took our daughters. In my anger, I sent my army to kill you. Limhi did not know anything about this. He said: I will search among my people and whoever has done this will be killed.

When Gideon, the king's captain, heard these things, he said to the king: I ask you to wait. Do not search this people. Do not blame them. Remember the priests of your father. They are in the wilderness. They are surely the ones who stole the Lamanite women. Tell them these things, so they will be calm towards us.

There are only a few of us and the Lamanites are coming with all their many armies. If their king does not settle them down, we will all be killed.

The words of Abinadi are being fulfilled, because we would not listen to the words of the Lord and repent. Let us put a stop to the shedding of so much blood.

Limhi told the Lamanite king all the things about his father and the priests that went into the wilderness. The king understood and said to them: Come with me without weapons to meet my armies and I promise that my people will not kill your people.

So they followed the king without weapons to meet the Lamanites. He bowed down before his armies and spoke for his people. When the Lamanites saw Limhi's people had no weapons, they had mercy on them and returned with their king peacefully to their own land.

Mosiah 21

Limhi and his people returned to the city of Nephi and lived in peace. But after some time, the Lamanites began to be stirred up again against the Nephites. They began to move into the borders of the land.

The Lamanites did not dare kill the people of Limhi, because of the promises that their king had made. But they would hit the people on their cheeks and boss them around and put heavy burdens on their backs and drive them as they would drive a stupid donkey.

The troubles of the Nephites were great and there was no way they could get out, for the Lamanites surrounded them on every side. The people began to complain to the king and wanted to go against the Lamanites in battle. They complained so much that the king told them to do what they wanted.

So they came together, put on their armor and went against the Lamanites. But the Lamanites beat them, pushed them back and killed many of them. There was a great howling and weeping among the people of Limhi.

There were many widows in the land. They cried from day to day in great fear. Their constant cries made the men of Limhi mad at the Lamanites. They went again to battle, but they were driven back again suffering much death. They battled again and suffered even more death.

Those who were not killed returned to the city of Nephi. They humbled themselves to the dust and allowed themselves to be slaves and be beaten and driven by their enemies. They humbled themselves in sadness. They prayed mightily to God all day long to save them from their hardships.

The Lord was slow to hear their cries because of their sins. After a time, the Lord heard their cries and began to soften the hearts of the Lamanites to ease their burdens. They began to prosper a little bit at a time and raise more grain, flocks and herds so they did not starve.

There were no more troubles between the Lamanites and the people of Limhi, even up to the time that Ammon and his brothers came into the land.

Limhi had his people watch for those priests who had stolen the daughters of the Lamanites. These priests came to their land at night to steal grain and many things.

The king was outside the city gates with his guards when they saw Ammon and his brothers coming. Limhi thought they were the hiding priests. This is why the king had Ammon tied and put into prison. When he learned they were his brothers from Zarahemla, he was filled with joy.

Ammon and his brothers were filled with sadness because so many of their brothers had been killed and because King Noah and his priests had caused the people to commit so many sins. They were sad Abinadi was killed.

They were sad that they did not know where to find Alma's people. Since the arrival of Ammon, King Limhi and many of his people promised God to serve him and keep his commandments. They now wanted to be baptized, but there was no one in the land with authority from God. Ammon would not do it because he felt he was not worthy. So they waited for the Holy Ghost to guide them.

The people wanted so much to become as Alma and his church, who had gone into the wilderness. They wanted to be baptized to show they were willing to serve God with all their hearts. But they had to wait. They also needed to find a way out of slavery to the Lamanites.

Mosiah 22

Ammon and the king gathered all the people together to find ideas on how to become free. But they could not think of a plan that would work.

Gideon said to the king: Remember the back gate at the back of the city. The Lamanites guards there are drunk every night. I will go there and pay the last tax of wine to them. When they are drunk and asleep, we will pass through. We can then leave with our women and our children and our flocks and herds into the wilderness.

King Limhi gathered his people together and sent plenty of wine to the Lamanite guards. When the guards were drunk and asleep, Limhi's people sneaked by night into the wilderness with their flocks and their herds. Ammon guided them into the wilderness towards the land of Zarahemla.

When the Lamanites learned that the people of Limhi had gone, they sent an army to bring them back. After two days, the army could not follow their tracks.

After many days, Ammon and the people of Limhi came to Zarahemla. They joined Mosiah's people. Mosiah welcomed them with joy. He also received their records and the records of the unknown people [Jaredites] that had been found in the wilderness.

Mosiah 23

The Lord blessed Alma's people. They came to a beautiful

land of pure water. The called the land Helam. They pitched their tents and began to farm the ground and build buildings.

They wanted Alma to be their king, for the people loved him. He said to them: It is not wise for us to have a king. If we could always have good kings, it would be good for us to have a king.

Remember the sins of King Noah and his priests. I myself was caught in their lies and we did many bad things. After much sadness, the Lord made me a tool in his hands to bring many of you to know his truth. But I do not glory, for I am unworthy of glory.

By God's power you are free from King Noah and from the bonds of sin. I hope you will keep your freedom. Trust no man to be your king. Trust no one to be your teacher or minister, unless he is a man of God and keeps his commandments.

Alma was their high priest and taught everyone to love his neighbor as himself. No one was given authority to preach or teach unless God told Alma to allow it. The teachers were all good men. They watched over their people and fed them with goodness.

The people grew rich. The Lord decided to test their patience and faith and show them that only God can save them. While they were farming the land, a Lamanite army came to the borders of their land. The men ran back from their fields and gathered in the city of Helam. The people were scared of the Lamanites.

Alma stood among them and told them to have courage. Their God would save them. So they hushed their fears and began to pray to the Lord to spare them, their wives and their children. And the Lord softened the hearts of the Lamanites. Alma and his brothers went and gave themselves and their lands to the Lamanites.

The Lamanite army had been lost in the wilderness from chasing Ammon and the people of Limhi. They found the priests of King Noah. The leader of the priests, Amulon, sent their stolen Lamanite wives to beg the army for mercy for their husbands.

The Lamanites did not kill them, but told them to join them in their search for a way back to the land of Nephi. On their way back home, they came upon Alma's people.

The Lamanite ruler promised Alma and his brothers that if they would show them the way back to the land of Nephi, they would not kill them, but give them freedom. After Alma showed them the way, the Lamanites did not keep their promise. They put guards around the land of Helam, over Alma and his brother.

The king made Amulon, the leader of Noah's priests, ruler over the people of Alma.

Mosiah 24

Amulon ruled over Alma and his brothers and abused them. He remembered Alma when he was one of Noah's priests. Amulon was angry with him and put burdens on them and put mean bosses over them. The people's hardships were so great they began to cry mightily to God. Amulon told them they should stop their prayers. He put guards over them to kill anyone who was caught praying to God.

So Alma and his people stopped praying out loud. They prayed to God in silence. The voice of the Lord came to them saying: Lift your heads and be of good comfort. I know the promise you have made to me; I promise to bring you out of slavery.

I will ease your burdens that you will not feel them on your backs. I will do this so you will know that I, the Lord God, will visit my people in their hardships.

So the slave work which Alma and his brothers were forced to do was made easy. The Lord gave them strength. They did, cheerfully and patiently, do the will of the Lord. Their faith and patience was great. The voice of the Lord came to them again, saying: Be happy, for tomorrow I will bring you out of slavery.

God said to Alma: Go before this people and I will go with you. So Alma and his people gathered their flocks and food in the night. In the morning, the Lord made a deep sleep come on the

Lamanites. Then Alma and his people escaped into the wilderness.

After they traveled all day, they pitched their tents in a valley. They named it Alma. All the men, all the women and all the children who could speak, lifted their voices in praise to God. They poured out thanks to God because he had been merciful to them, eased their burdens and gave them freedom.

The Lord said to Alma: Arise and get this people out of this land. The Lamanites have awakened and they now chase after you. Get out of this land and I will stop the Lamanites in this valley so they cannot chase you.

After twelve days of walking, they arrived in the land of Zarahemla where King Mosiah welcomed them with joy.

Mosiah 25

King Mosiah gathered the people of Zarahemla and the people of Limhi and the people of Alma and he read to them the stories of Zeniff. He also read the stories of Alma and his brothers.

When Mosiah finished reading, his people were full of wonder and amazement. They did not know how to feel. When they saw those who had been made free, they were filled with great joy. But when they thought of their brothers who had been killed, they were filled with sadness.

When they thought of the immediate goodness of God and His power, they raised their voices and gave thanks to God. When they thought of the evil of the Lamanites, they were filled with pain and worry for their souls.

King Mosiah asked Alma to form churches in the land. Mosiah gave Alma power to ordain priests and teachers over every church. The Lord poured out his Spirit on them.

Mosiah 26

There were many of the rising generation that did not believe what had been said about the resurrection of the dead. They also did not believe in the coming of Christ. They would not be baptized or join the church.

They were not half as many as the people of God, but they did cause many others to commit sins. Those in the church who committed sin were brought to the leaders of the church. Alma was troubled in his spirit; he feared he would do the wrong thing. So he asked the Lord what he should do.

After he had poured out his whole soul to God, the voice of the Lord came to him, saying: Blessed are you, Alma. Blessed are those who were baptized in the waters of Mormon. Blessed are these people who carry my name, for they are mine.

You will judge anyone who sins against me. If they confess their sins and repent, you will forgive them. Yes, as often as my people repent, I will forgive them. But those who will not repent will not be members of my church.

After Alma heard these words, he went and judged those who sinned against God. Those who repented were kept in the church. Those that would not confess their sins and repent were no longer members of the church and their names were erased.

Alma and his fellow teachers suffered all kinds of trouble from those who were not of the church of God. But they still gave thanks to God in all things.

Mosiah 27

The insults by the unbelievers became so great that many church members began to whisper complaints. King Mosiah sent a letter saying that all people should be equal and telling nonbelievers to stop bothering church members. There began to be peace again in the land. The people began to be numerous building large cities and villages in all parts of the land. The Lord visited them and blessed them to be a large and wealthy people.

But the sons of Mosiah joined the nonbelievers. Alma, the son of Alma, became a wicked man. He was a man who spoke many powerful words. He led many of the people to sin. He went secretly with the sons of Mosiah trying to destroy the church and lead away the people of the Lord.

As they were traveling, an angel of the Lord appeared. The angel spoke with a voice of thunder that made the ground shake. They were so scared they fell to the ground.

The angel said: Alma, why do you trouble the church of God? The Lord hears the prayers of his people and his servant, Alma, your father. Your father has prayed with much faith for you. Because of his faith, the Lord has spared you and sent me to show you His power.

Can you see me before you? I am sent from God. Does not my voice shake the earth? Can you still argue against the power of God? I say to you, Alma, do not try to destroy the church. These were the last words that the angel spoke to Alma. Then the angel departed.

Alma and the sons of Mosiah fell again to the earth; great was their fear. They had seen an angel. His voice was like thunder; it shook the earth. They knew only God's power could shake the earth like it was going to shake apart.

Alma was so shocked that he could not speak, or even open his mouth. He became so weak that he could not move his hands. He was carried to his father and laid down.

His father was happy, for he knew that this was the power of God. He gathered the people together so they could see what the Lord had done for his son. After they had fasted and prayed for two days and nights, Alma the younger stood and began to speak.

He said: I have repented of my sins and have been saved by the Lord. I am born of the Spirit. The Lord said to me: Do not wonder that all people must be born again. Yes, born of God, they are changed from their sinful condition to a state of good. They are saved by God and become new. Only then can they inherit God's kingdom.

I have been in the darkness. My soul was racked with terrible pain. I had rejected Christ the Lord. After wading through misery, almost to death, the Lord in mercy brought me out of the awful chains of sin. Now I know Christ will come and that He remembers every person. Every knee will bow and every tongue will say that He is God.

From this day on, Alma and four of the sons of Mosiah, Ammon, Aaron, Omner and Himni, who were with Alma at the time the angel appeared to them, traveled through all the land preaching the word of God.

Unbelievers often beat them. Still, they tried to repair the damage they did to the people of the church. They became tools in the hands of God to bring many people to God. They were blessed, for they spread peace and showed the people that the Lord rules.

Mosiah 28

After the sons of Mosiah did these things, they went to the land of Nephi to share the word of God with the Lamanites, for they could not bear any soul to suffer in sin and ignorance.

None of King Mosiah's sons wanted to be king. So he took the plates of brass and all the things which he had kept and gave them to Alma the younger.

Mosiah 29

Mosiah sent a letter to his people, saying: O my people, I say that you should have no king. Many people have sinned because of their kings. You should select judges to rule by our laws.

People usually choose right, so you should make your own laws by the voice of the people. Then, if people choose sins, the sins will come on their own heads. I want this land to be a land of liberty and equality. Let everyone enjoy equal rights and privileges.

After King Mosiah said these words, the people stopped wanting a king. They became eager for every person to have an equal vote. They organized into groups to vote for judges.

They voted Alma the younger to be the first chief judge. Alma kept God's commandments and judged fairly. Thus began the rule of the judges. There was peace throughout the land. The people became joyful because of their freedom.

Alma the older and King Mosiah died. The people had a strong love for Mosiah. They loved him more than they loved any other man. He had not taken riches from them and he made peace in the land.

ALMA
Son of Alma

Alma 1

In the first year of the judges, a large, strong man, named Nehor, taught the people not to fear God. Many people believed Nehor and gave him money. He was proud and wore fancy clothes.

Gideon was an older man. He had helped free Limhi's people from slavery. One day Nehor argued with Gideon. Then Nehor killed Gideon with his sword.

Nehor was taken to Alma to be judged for murder. Nehor begged to live. Alma said: You have killed a man who did much good for the people. If we spare you, your guilt will come on us.

They took Nehor to the top of the hill Manti to be killed. Before he died, Nehor told the people he had been teaching lies.

But many people loved fancy things. They taught religion for money. They wanted riches. The true followers of Christ taught God's word for free.

In the Church of God, the teacher is no better than the learner. All are equal and both the teacher and hearer do work. They shared with the poor and the needy and the sick. They dressed neat and pleasing, but did not wear fancy clothes.

God blessed them to become rich. They had plenty of flocks and herds, grain, gold and silver and silk and fine fabric. They did not send away anyone that was poor, or hungry, or thirsty, or sick.

They did not put their hearts on riches. They were generous to old and young, male and female, church members and nonmembers.

They become more wealthy than people who did not belong to their church. Many who did not belong to the church were lazy. They were lifted up in pride, lying, stealing, robbing and murdering.

People who broke the law were punished. This helped keep the wicked quiet. There was peace among the people of Nephi until the fifth year of the judges.

Alma 2

In the fifth year there was a sneaky man named Amlici. With tricky words, he became powerful. He wanted to be king. This upset the people of the church. They knew that if Amlici became king, he would take away their rights. Amlici wanted to destroy the Church of God.

One day all the people came together to vote for or against Amlici. Most of the people voted against Amlici.

But Amlici stirred up his people to anger. They said Amlici was their king. He told his followers to fight against the rest of the people.

The people of Amlici were called Amlicites. The rest of the people were called Nephites, or the people of God.

The Amlicites wanted to kill them. The Nephites prepared with swords, bows, arrows, stones, slings and all kinds of weapons.

The Amlicites came near the river Sidon to war. Alma fought at the front of his armies against the Amlicites. They began to battle on the hill east of Sidon.

The Amlicites fought with great strength and killed many of the Nephites, but the Lord gave strength to the Nephites. The Amlicites began to run away.

The Nephites chased them all day and killed twelve thousand five hundred thirty two Amlicites. Six thousand five hundred sixty two Nephites were killed.

When Alma could no longer chase the Amlicites, he had his

people put up their tents in the valley of Gideon. The valley was called Gideon, in honor of the man who was killed by Nehor.

Alma sent spies to follow the Amlicites. In the morning, the spies came running fast back into camp. They were so scared, saying: We followed them and to our great surprise, we saw a great army of Lamanites.

The Amlicites joined them. They are killing our brothers, sisters and children in that land. Now they are coming to our city, Zarahemla. If we do not hurry, they will take our city. Our wives and children will be killed.

The army of Nephi ran toward their city. As they were crossing the river Sidon, the Lamanite and Amlicite warriors were as many as the sands of the sea.

The Amlicites had painted their foreheads red like the Lamanites. The heads of the Lamanites were shaved. The Nephites began to pray mightily for God to save them. The Lord gave them strength.

Alma fought face to face with Amlici. Alma cried out: O Lord, have mercy and spare my life, that I may be a tool in your hands to save this people. When Alma said these words, he struggled again with Amlici and killed him with the sword.

Then Alma fought the Lamanite king, but he ran away, sending his guards to kill Alma. Alma and his guards killed them and pushed them back to a part of the land that is full of wild, hungry beasts. Many Lamanites and Amlicites were eaten by wild animals and by vultures. Their bones are found in large piles.

Alma 3

There were too many dead people to count. The bodies of the Lamanites and Amlicites were thrown into the river and their bones washed away to sea.

Many Nephite women and children were killed. Many of their flocks and herds were destroyed. The marching armies smashed down many fields of grain. After they finished burying their dead, the Nephites returned to their lands and families.

In this year, tens of thousands of people were killed, both good and bad. They are gone to the eternal world for eternal joy or eternal sadness, according to the spirit they chose to obey.

Alma 4

In the sixth year of judges, the people were still sad for their killed brothers, husbands and fathers. They believed war was a punishment sent from God because of their sins. Many people repented and were baptized in the river Sidon.

In the eighth year of judges, the people of the church began to grow proud because of their riches. They had fine clothes, many herds and much gold and silver. They began to wear fancy clothes.

This made Alma and many of the church leaders worry. They were sad about the sins they saw.

Church members began to put their hearts on riches. They began to be mean to each other. They began to beat people who did not believe. Their envy and pride was even more than the people who did not belong to the church. The Church began to fail.

The members' bad example began to lead nonmembers to sin. Alma saw great inequality among the people. Some turned their backs on the needy and the hungry and the thirsty and the sick.

This was cause for great shame and sadness among the people. Some people were humble and helped others. Alma saw the hardships that were put on the humble followers of God by the rest of his people.

He selected a wise man, named Nephihah to take Alma's place as chief judge. Alma could then go to his people and remind them of their duties. Alma used God's word to pull them down from their pride.

Alma 5

These are the words that Alma spoke to the people of the church in Zarahemla: I ask you, have you spiritually been born of God? Do you have his image in your face? Have you felt a mighty change in your hearts? Can you see yourself standing before God to be judged for your actions? Can you look to God with a pure heart and clean hands?

Can you imagine the voice of the Lord, saying to you: Come to me; your works have been good? Do you think you can lie to the Lord in that day?

Imagine being brought to stand before God with your soul filled with guilt and regret. You cannot think of being saved when you have followed the devil. Such persons cannot have a place in the kingdom of heaven. They will be thrown out.

Have you kept yourself innocent before God? Can you say that you are humble? Are you empty of pride? If you are not, you are not prepared to meet God. Are you empty of envy? Do you make fun of others? If you do, you are not prepared to meet God.

Repent, repent, for the Lord God has spoken it! His arms of mercy reach out to all people. He says: Repent and I will accept you. He says: Come to me and you will enjoy the fruit of the tree of life. You will never be thrown out.

The Good Shepherd calls you. Listen to the voice of the Good Shepherd; follow Him. But if you do evil, you are listening to the devil and following him.

I promise you these things are true. How do you think that I know? I have fasted and prayed many days so I could know them. The Holy Spirit of God has told them to me.

Jesus Christ will come. The Son of our Heavenly Father is full of mercy and truth. He will come to pay for the sins of the world; yes, for the sins of every man who steadily believes in Him.

I ask you, how can you push away God's words. How can you be puffed up in pride? Will you continue to wear fancy clothes and put your hearts on your riches? Will you keep thinking you are better than others? Will you keep turning away from the poor?

If you want to follow the Good Shepherd, come away from evil. The Good Shepherd calls to you. If you listen to His voice, you are His sheep. He will bring you into His flock. He will watch over you. A shepherd does not allow wolves to come into his flock.

I command you people of the Church to obey my words. People who do not belong to the Church, I invite you to obey. Come, repent and be baptized that you too may enjoy the fruit of the tree of life.

Alma 6

Alma ordained priests to watch over the Church. God's word was open to all. No one was kept from hearing it. Alma went to the land of Gideon to teach about Jesus Christ.

Alma 7

Alma said: I have come with great hope to find you humbled before God and not in the awful situation that our brothers were in at Zarahemla.

God has told me they are back on the path of goodness. I have joy in them again.

I trust I will also have joy in you. I trust you believe in God. I trust you are not lifted up in pride. I trust you do not put your hearts on riches. I trust you worship the true and living God and you look forward to forgiveness.

Jesus Christ will soon live on the earth. He will suffer pains and temptations of every kind. He will overcome death and take on Him the sins of His people.

You must repent and be born again. Come and be baptized to wash away your sins. Have faith in the Lamb of God. He is mighty to save. Show God you are willing to be baptized. Promise that you will keep His commandments. If you are baptized and keep God's commandments, you will have eternal life.

I know you believe these things. You are in the path that leads to the kingdom of God. My joy in you is great. Be humble. Be gentle and easy to be asked. Be full of patience and long-suffering. Be moderate in all things. Keep God's commandments at all times.

Ask God for what you need, both for your mind and body. Always return thanks to God for the things you are given. Have faith, hope and charity, then you will have good works. May the Lord bless you for your faith and good works, from this time and forever. Amen.

Alma 8

Alma then returned to his house in Zarahemla to rest. Next, he went to the land of Melek and baptized people throughout the land. Alma then traveled three days to a city called Ammonihah.

Satan held their hearts. They would not listen. Alma wrestled in mighty prayer with God for the people in this city, but they would not soften their hearts.

They said to him: We know you are Alma the high priest over the Church. We are not of your church. We do not believe in your foolish ideas. We know you have no power over us.

They spit on Alma and threw him out of their city. Alma went away to the next city. He was weighed down with great sadness, because of the sins of the people of Ammonihah. An angel of the Lord came to him, saying: Blessed are you, Alma. Lift up your head and have joy. You have great reason to be happy. You have obeyed God's commandments from the time you were given the first message from him.

Return to Ammonihah. Preach again to the people. They are planning to destroy your people. Tell them that if they do not repent, the Lord will destroy them.

So Alma returned speedily to Ammonihah. He entered the city by another way. He said to a man: Will you give a humble servant of God something to eat?

The man said to him: I am Amulek, a Nephite. I know you are a holy prophet of God. An angel told me to look for you. Come in my house; I will share my food.

When Alma was full, he blessed Amulek and his house and gave thanks to God. Alma stayed many days with Amulek before Alma began to preach to the people.

The people were growing more evil. God's word came to Alma, saying: Take Amulek and prophesy to this people. Tell them: If you do not repent, you will be destroyed.

Filled with the Holy Ghost, Alma and Amulek went teaching the people. They were given power. No jail could hold them. No one could kill them. This was done so the Lord could show His power in them.

Alma 9

The people began to argue with Alma, saying: Who do you think you are? Do you think we will believe the word of one man who says that this great city will be destroyed in one day? Who is this God that sends a single man to this people to say such things?

They tried to grab Alma, but they could not hold him. Alma spoke to them boldly, saying: You wicked people, so soon you forget God's commandments.

Can you remember our father, Lehi, who came out of Jerusalem by the hand of God? Can you remember that God led them through the wilderness? Have you forgotten so soon the many times God saved our fathers from their enemies? If it had not been for God's great mercy and long-suffering to us, we would have been killed long ago.

Repent or you will be destroyed. God says: If you keep my commandments, you will be blessed. If you do not keep my commandments, you will be cut off.

In the Day of Judgment, it will be more merciful for them than for you, if you remain in your sins. Their sins come from not knowing truth and from the evil traditions of their fathers. The Lord will be merciful to them.

Your time in the land will not be long. If you, who receive so many blessings from the Lord, continue to go against the light and knowledge that you have, the Lamanites will be sent on you. They will come in a time when you know not and they will destroy you.

When I, Alma, spoke these words, the people were angry because I said they were a stubborn and fallen people. They tried to grab me to put me in prison, but the Lord's power stopped them.

Alma 10

Then Amulek stood and said: I am Amulek, son of Giddonah. I am a man of good reputation among all who know me. I have many relatives and friends. I have many riches from my hard work.

I did not know much about God. He called me many times, but I had hardened my heart. Even though I knew about the Lord, I did not want to know. I ignored God until the fourth day of this month.

As I was walking, an angel of the Lord came to me and said: Amulek, return to your house. You must feed a prophet of the Lord, a holy man chosen by God. He has not eaten for many days and he is hungry.

Take him into your house and feed him. He will bless you and your house; and the blessing of the Lord will rest on you and your house.

I, Amulek, obeyed the voice of the angel and returned to my house. As I was going there, I found the man whom the angel spoke about.

Alma blessed me, my wife, my children, my father and relatives. The Lord's blessing rested on us. I know the things Alma speaks of are true. While he stayed at my house, God sent an angel to make these things clear to me.

When Amulek spoke these words, the people began to be amazed. They now saw more than one witness for God. But lawyers wanted to trick them in their words. These lawyers were educated and clever.

Amulek knew their thoughts. He said to them: You wicked lawyers and hypocrites, you are working for the devil. You are laying traps with words to catch the holy ones of God. If not for the prayers of the good people, you would already be destroyed.

Now the people were more angry. Amulek stretched out his hand and said even mightier to them: You wicked people. Why do you let Satan get such great hold on your hearts? Why will you give him power over you to blind your eyes to the truth?

The people yelled out against him. Zeezrom, one of the lawyers, accused Amulek and Alma of breaking the law.

Alma 11

Their judges and lawyers often stirred up trouble in order to get more work and more money. Zeezrom said to Amulek: I will give you six onties of silver [about three months' pay] if you will deny there is a God.

Amulek said: You know there is a God, but you love money.

Zeezrom asked again: Do you say that God's Son will come? Amulek answered: Yes.

Zeezrom said: Shall He save His people in their sins? Amulek answered: He will not.

Then Zeezrom said to the people: See, he says that the Son of God will come, but not save His people.

Amulek then said: You have lied. I said He will not save His people in their sins. Jesus Christ cannot save people in their sins. No unclean thing can enter the kingdom of heaven. He only saves people who repent.

Zeezrom changed the subject and asked Amulek: Is the Son of God the Eternal Father? Amulek said: Yes, he is the Eternal Father of heaven and of earth and of our salvation.

Our bodies will die, but Christ will overcome death.

Because of Him, our spirit and our body will join again in perfect health. Not one hair of our heads will be lost. This resurrection will come to all, both old and young, both slave and free, male and female, evil and good.

Then we will live forever and be brought before Christ the Son, God the Father and the Holy Spirit to be judged for the good and evil we have done.

When Amulek finished speaking, the people were amazed. Zeezrom was afraid and trembled.

Alma 12

Zeezrom was convinced more and more of God's power. He said to Alma: What is resurrection of the dead, when both good and evil people must stand before God to be judged?

Alma explained: People may know God's mysteries. People who open their hearts are given more knowledge about God, until they know all His mysteries.

But people who harden their hearts lose their knowledge about God, until they know nothing about Him. They are taken by the devil and led to destruction. These are the chains of hell.

Our evil words can stop us; our evil works can stop us and our evil thoughts can stop us. Evil people will not even want to look at God. But this cannot be; we must all stand before God in His glory and power and confess our sins. Then a second death will come to evil people. It is a spiritual death. They will be put away from God.

When Alma finished speaking, the people began to be amazed. But Antionah, a chief ruler, said to him: What is this you have said? He asked: How can a person rise from the dead and be changed to never die? Man cannot live forever.

Alma said: This life is the time to prepare to meet God. He gave us commandments, and freedom to choose to obey or disobey. After we die, we will come alive again and our lives will be judged.

Alma 13

Humble yourselves. Repent. You have the scriptures. If you ignore them, you will be destroyed. Alma stretched out his hand and spoke with a mighty voice: Now is the time to repent. The day of salvation is near.

The Lord speaks His voice to all nations so all people may have great joy. He sends His glad message to people over the whole earth. His words are given to us plainly. Angels are sharing His words right now to many people in our land.

We are waiting to hear the joyful news of the birth of Jesus Christ to earth. The time is coming; we do not know how soon. Angels will tell it to good and holy people.

I wish from the inmost part of my heart that you will listen to my words. Throw off your sins. Do not delay the day of your repentance.

Watch and pray continually so you will not be tempted more than you can stand. Be led by the Holy Spirit. Be full of love and long-suffering. Have faith in the Lord. Have hope that you will have eternal life.

Alma 14

Many of the people believed Alma's words. They began to repent and search the scriptures.

But most of the people wanted to kill Alma and Amulek. The angry people grabbed them and tied them with strong ropes. They were taken to the chief judge. The people said many lies about them to the judge.

Zeezrom, the lawyer, said: I am guilty, not Alma and Amulek. These men are spotless before God.

Zeezrom begged the judge to spare Alma and Amulek. Now the people hated Zeezrom, too. They spit on him. They threw him out with all the others who believed in Alma and Amulek.

The angry crowd took the believers and their wives and children and threw them into a fire. They carried Alma and Amulek to the fire to make them watch the people die.

When Amulek saw the pains of the women and children in the fire, he said to Alma: How can we watch this awful scene? Let us stretch our hands and use the power of God that is in us to save them from the flames.

Alma said: The Holy Spirit stops me. The Lord will take them up to Himself in glory. God allows this to happen so the blood of the innocent will stand against the murderers.

Amulek said: Maybe we will be burned, too. Alma said: Our work is not finished, so they cannot kill us.

The chief judge hit them in their faces and said to them: After what you have seen, will you still preach to this people and have them thrown into a lake of fire? You do not have power to save them. Your God did not save them.

Then the judge hit Alma and Amulek again and asked: What do say you for yourselves? Alma and Amulek would not answer, so the judge hit them and put them into prison.

Three days later, many lawyers, judges, priests and teachers came in the prison to see them. They asked many questions, but Alma and Amulek did not answer.

A judge stood in front of them and asked: Why do you not answer their questions? Do you not know I have the power to burn you in the flames? He commanded them to speak; but Alma and Amulek would not answer.

The next day, more people came and hit Alma and Amulek and said: If you have such great power, why do you not save yourselves? The people bit them and spit on them, saying: How will we look when we are sent to hell?

They made fun of the prophets for many days. They took away their clothes, tied them with strong ropes and would not give them food or water.

The chief judge came back and beat them. He said to them: If you have God's power, save yourselves. Then we will believe your words. People took turns hitting them.

Then the power of God was with Alma and Amulek. They stood on their feet and Alma cried out to heaven: How long will we suffer these terrible pains, O Lord? Give us strength to be made free by our faith in Christ.

Then Alma and Amulek broke free from the strong ropes. When the people saw this, they began to run away. But they were so afraid they fell on the floor and could not even crawl.

The earth began to shake mightily and the walls of the prison fell down. The chief judge, the lawyers, the priests and the teachers who hit Alma and Amulek were all killed by the falling walls. Alma and Amulek walked out of the prison. The Lord gave them power, by their faith in Christ.

When the people of the city heard the great noise, they came running to see what happened. They saw Alma and Amulek coming out of the prison and the prison fallen to the earth.

The people became scared. They ran away from Alma and Amulek like goats running from two lions. But the people of Ammonihah would still not repent.

Alma 15

God told Alma and Amulek to leave. As they traveled, they found the people who were thrown out and stoned because they believed in Alma's words.

Zeezrom became sick with a burning fever made by the guilt of his sins. He thought Alma and Amulek were killed and he blamed himself. When he heard that Alma and Amulek had escaped, his heart took courage.

When Zeezrom saw them, he asked Alma and Amulek to heal him. Alma said: Do you believe in the power of Christ? Zeezrom answered: Yes, I believe all the words you have taught. Then Alma said: If you believe in Christ, you can be healed. O Lord our God, have mercy on this man and heal him according to his faith in Christ.

When Alma said these words, Zeezrom leaped to his feet and began to walk. This amazed all the people.

Alma baptized Zeezrom and all who wanted to be baptized. There were many; people flocked in from all around the land.

Amulek gave up all his gold and silver for God's word and he went with Alma to Zarahemla. But Amulek's friends, father, and relatives rejected him.

Alma 16

In the eleventh year, the cry of war came on the city of Ammonihah. The armies of the Lamanites began to kill the people and destroy the city. Before the Nephites could gather an army, the wicked people of Ammonihah were destroyed. Yes, every living soul of the Ammonihahites was killed. Their great city, which they said was too great for God to destroy, was left empty in one day.

Dogs and wild beasts ate their bodies. After many days, their dead bodies were piled up and covered with dirt. The smell was so bad that no one was willing to live in Ammonihah for many years.

For the next three years, the people of Nephi had peace in all the land. Alma and Amulek preached in the temples and churches, which were built like Jewish churches.

Church members spread throughout the land of the Nephites. Everyone was fair with each other, so the Lord poured out His Spirit on all. The Spirit prepared their minds and hearts to hear God's word with joy.

They learned the Lord would show himself to them after His resurrection. This gave the people great joy.

Alma 17

As Alma traveled, he met his friends the sons of Mosiah. They were returning to Zarahemla. They were with Alma when the angel came to him. Alma was glad his friends still loved the Lord.

Mosiah's sons had grown strong in truth. They had searched the scriptures carefully. This is not all. They had prayed and fasted much. They had the spirit of prophecy and revelation. They taught with God's power and authority.

For fourteen years they taught the Lamanites and brought many to God. They had many hardships; they suffered great hunger, thirst and tiredness.

This is their story: When Mosiah was nearing death, his sons refused to be king. Instead, they went to the Lamanites to preach the gospel. The sons of Mosiah hunted for food on the way with spears, bows, arrows and slings.

The Lord visited them with His Spirit and said: Go to the Lamanites and teach my word. Be patient in suffering and hardships. Be good examples and I will make you tools in my hands to save many souls.

The sons of Mosiah and the people who were with them took courage. When they arrived in the borders of the Lamanites, they went in different ways. They trusted the Lord would someday bring them together again. They knew they were beginning a great work.

They preached God's word to a wild and mean people who enjoyed murdering and robbing Nephites. The Lamanites loved riches, gold, silver and costly things. They tried to become rich by murdering and stealing so they did not have to work. They were lazy.

The sons of Mosiah taught one person at a time. Ammon went to the land of Ishmael. The Lamanites tied him and took him to the King Lamoni.

The king asked Ammon if he wanted to live with his people. Ammon said: Yes, I want to live here maybe for the rest of my life. I will be your servant.

King Lamoni was pleased. He sent Ammon with other servants to watch his flocks. One day as they were taking the king's animals to water, another group of Lamanites came and chased the animals away.

The servants began to moan and cry, saying: Now the king

will kill us. He killed our brothers when their flocks were scattered by these evil men.

When Ammon saw this his heart was lifted in joy. He thought he could win the hearts of these servants by saving the flocks. He said to them: My brothers, be of good cheer. Let us go search for the flocks. We will gather them together. The king will not kill us.

The evil men came back to scatter their flocks. Ammon threw stones at them with his sling. He killed some of the evil men. The others became angry and came to Ammon to kill him with clubs.

When they lifted their clubs to kill him, Ammon raised his sword with great power and cut off their arms. Even though there were many men, they became afraid of Ammon. They ran away from him.

After he chased them off, the king's servants watered the flocks and returned to the king. They carried the many arms Ammon had cut off.

Alma 18

They told the king about Ammon's faithfulness and great power. The king was amazed. He said: Ammon is more than a man. Is he the Great Spirit?

They answered: We know he cannot be killed and we know he is a friend of the king.

The king asked: Where is this man who has such power? They said: He is feeding your horses. When the king heard Ammon was feeding the horses, he was even more amazed by Ammon's work.

The king said: This man is the most loyal person. He must be the Great Spirit. I want him to come to me, but I do not dare ask.

The king's servant said to Ammon: Rabbanah (which means powerful king) our king wants you to stay. Ammon came and said to the king: What do you want me to do for you, O King?

The king was afraid to answer for one hour. Ammon was filled with God's Spirit; he knew the king's thoughts. Ammon said: Why are you amazed? I am your servant. Whatever you ask me to do, which is right, I will do.

The king asked: Who are you? Are you that Great Spirit who knows all things? Ammon answered: I am not.

The king said: How do you know my heart? By what power did you fight the attackers. If you will tell me these things, I will give you anything you ask.

Ammon was wise and kind. He said: This is what I ask; listen to my words. The king said: Yes, I will listen and believe all your words.

Ammon began to speak: Do you believe that the Great Spirit, who is God, created all things on earth and in heaven? Lamoni said: Yes, I believe he created all things on earth, but I know nothing about a heaven.

Ammon said to him: Heaven is the place where God lives. God sees all people. He knows their thoughts and wishes. He created you, too.

King Lamoni said: I believe all the things you say. Are you sent from God? Ammon answered: God's Holy Spirit sent me to teach this people. His Spirit gives me great knowledge and power.

Then Ammon taught the king about the Holy Scriptures from the creation of the earth to the time their father, Lehi, left Jerusalem. Ammon taught the gospel plan, the coming of Christ and all the works of the Lord.

The king believed and began to pray to the Lord, saying: Lord, have mercy on me and my people. When he said this, the king fainted to the ground.

His servants carried him to his wife and laid him on a bed. He was still, as if he were dead, for two days and two nights. His wife, sons and daughters cried over him.

Alma 19

When they were about to take the king's body and bury it, the queen sent for Ammon. She said to him: The king's servants told me you are a prophet of God and that you have power to do mighty works in his name. Some say my husband is still alive; others say he is dead, that he stinks and should be buried. To me, he does not stink.

Ammon knew the king was not dead. King Lamoni was under the power of God. The light of Christ had overcome the king's natural strength. Ammon said: The king will wake tomorrow; do not bury him.

Ammon asked the queen: Do you believe this? She said: I have no proof other than your word and the word of our servants, but I believe what you say. Ammon said to her: Blessed are you because of your faith.

The queen stayed with her husband and he did awake. He arose and stretched his hand to his wife and said: Blessed is God and blessed are you. I have seen my Lord. He will come and save all who believe in him.

When he said these words, his heart was filled with joy and he fainted again. The Spirit also overcame the queen and she fainted. When Ammon saw the Spirit of the Lord was poured out on the Lamanites, he was overcome with joy. Ammon also fainted to the ground.

When the king's servants saw that all three had fallen, they prayed to the Lord with all their might. They, too, were overcome and fainted, all except one woman whose name was Abish.

Abish had believed in the Lord for many years. She had seen a great vision, but she told no one about it. When she saw that the servants, the queen and king, and Ammon, had fainted to the ground, she knew it was God's power. She thought this would help people believe in God, so she ran from house to house telling everyone.

Many people came to the king's house. The crowd was amazed when they saw the king and the queen and their servants laying on the earth.

Some blamed Ammon. One of them, whose brother had been killed by Ammon, was still angry. He wanted to kill Ammon, but as he lifted his sword, he fell dead by the power of God.

When the crowds saw the man fall dead, fear came on them all. They did not dare touch Ammon or any who had fallen. They began to wonder among themselves what all these things could mean.

While they were talking, the woman servant took the queen by the hand. As soon as she touched her hand, the queen arose and stood on her feet and said in a loud voice: O blessed Jesus, you have saved me from an awful hell! O blessed God, have mercy on this people!

She said this in great joy and took the king by the hand. He stood on his feet. He began to teach the people the words that Ammon taught.

All those who listened to the king were converted to the Lord. But many would not listen and went on their way.

When the king's servants rose up, they said their hearts had been changed. They had no more desire to do evil. They said they had seen and talked with angels. Ammon rose up, too.

Many of the people believed and were baptized. They became a good people and they formed a church. In this way, the Lord began his work among the Lamanites.

The Lord began to pour out His Spirit on them. We see that God gives His love and mercy to all who repent and believe in Him.

Alma 20-21

King Lamoni asked Ammon to go meet his father, the king of the Lamanites. But the Lord told Ammon: Do not go; the king will try to kill you. Go to the land of Middoni. Your brothers Aaron, Muloki and Ammah are in prison there. Ammon said to

Lamoni: My brothers are in prison at Middoni. I must rescue them.

Lamoni said: Who told you your brothers were in prison? Ammon said: God told me. Then Lamoni said: I know you can do all things by the Lord's strength. I will go with you; the king of Middoni is my friend.

As Ammon and Lamoni traveled, they met Lamoni's father, the king of all the Lamanites. He said to Lamoni: I made a feast for my sons and for my people. Why did you not come? Where are you going with this Nephite liar?

When Lamoni told his father where he was going, his father was angry and said: Lamoni, these Nephite liars are here to trick you and steal your riches. I tell you to kill Ammon. Lamoni said to him: I will not kill Ammon. I will go to Middoni to rescue God's holy prophets.

When his father heard these words, he was angry at Lamoni. He raised his sword to kill his own son. But Ammon stood in the way and said: You will not kill your son, even though it would be better for him to be killed than you. He has repented of his sins.

The king answered: You are the one I should kill. You tried to destroy my son. Then the king tried to kill Ammon, but Ammon hit the king's arm so hard he could not lift it.

Ammon raised his sword over the king. The king was afraid and said: Spare me and I will give you whatever you ask, even half of my kingdom. Ammon said: Just let my brothers out of prison and let Lamoni keep his kingdom.

When the king saw Ammon had great love for his son Lamoni, he was amazed. He said: I will release your brothers. I will allow my son Lamoni to rule his kingdom forever. Bring your brothers and teach me the words you have taught my son.

Ammon's brothers were let out of prison. They had no clothes. Their skins were bleeding and torn, they had been tied for so long with strong ropes. They had suffered hunger, thirst and pain. Still, they had been patient. They were given food and clothes.

Alma 22

Aaron and his brothers went to the king of the Lamanites and bowed down before him and said: O king, we are Ammon's brothers, whom you rescued from prison.

The king said: I am troubled because of Ammon's kindness and great words. Rise and teach me. What is the Spirit of the Lord? Why did Ammon say: If you repent, you will be saved; if you do not repent, you will be thrown off?

Aaron answered: Do you believe that there is a God? The king said: I know the Amalekites say there is a God. I let them build churches to worship him. If you say there is a God, I will believe. Is God that Great Spirit who brought our fathers from Jerusalem? Aaron said: Yes, he is the Great Spirit. He created all things.

The king believed and asked: What should I do to have this eternal life and be filled with joy at the last day? I will give up all I have for it.

Aaron said: Bow down before God and repent of all your sins. Call on his name in faith. Then you will have the hope you want.

The king bowed down and prayed mightily, saying: O God, Aaron told me there is a God. If there is a God and if you are God, will you make yourself known to me. I will give away my sins to know you and be saved.

When the king said these words, he fainted to the ground. His servants ran and told the queen all that had happened. When she saw the king, he looked as if he were dead. She saw Aaron and his brothers standing as though they were to blame. She was angry with them. She told her servants to kill them, but the servants did not dare touch Aaron or his brothers.

Aaron then put his hand on the king and said: Stand. And the king stood. When the queen saw this, she began to fear. The king stood and calmed them and taught them.

Alma 23

The Lamanite king sent a letter to all his people saying that Ammon, Aaron, Omner, Himni and any of their brothers should be allowed to teach in the people's homes and churches.

Then Aaron and his brothers went from city to city and from church to church teaching and ordaining teachers to all the Lamanites.

The king allowed them to teach God's word wherever they wanted. They were led by the Holy Spirit to preach God's word in all of the Amalekites' churches. The Lord blessed them and they brought many people to the truth.

Thousands were brought to the Lord. All the Lamanites who believed never fell away from God. They became good and put down their weapons.

The king and all the believers were no longer called Lamanites, they became known as the Anti-Nephi-Lehites. They were friendly with the Nephites and God's curse was off them.

Alma 24

When the king died, he gave his kingdom to his son named Anti-Nephi-Lehi. The Lamanites who would not believe in the Lord did not want him to rule them. They took up weapons to fight the people of Anti-Nephi-Lehi. But the Anti-Nephi-Lehites would not fight, not even one of them.

King Anti-Nephi-Lehi told his people: I thank God for sending our brothers, the Nephites, to us. I thank God that he allows us to repent and be forgiven of our many sins and murders. Since God has washed away the stains from our swords, we cannot afford to stain them again.

God told me that if we stain our swords again he will not wash them clean. God has mercy on us, because he loves us. Let us hide our swords to show him we will not kill again. Bury them deep. If our brothers kill us, we will go to God and we will be saved.

When the king said these things, the people buried their swords and all their weapons deep in the ground. They did this to show God they would rather give up their own lives than kill again.

The unbelieving Lamanites sent their armies to kill the people of Anti-Nephi-Lehi. The people went and laid down on the ground in front of the Lamanite armies.

The Lamanites began to kill them with the sword. They killed one thousand and five. Then the Lamanites became amazed that the Anti-Nephi-Lehites would not run or turn away. They would lie down, be killed and even praise God while they were being killed.

The Lamanites stopped killing and threw down their weapons. Their hearts became filled with mercy. They remembered their own sins.

Many Lamanites joined the people of the Lord, even more than the number of Anti-Nephi-Lehites who had been killed. We believe those who died went to God. The Lord works in many ways to save his children.

Alma 25

The Lamanites who were not converted blamed their murders on the Nephites. They left the Anti-Nephi-Lehites and took their armies to battle the Nephites. The Nephites pushed the Lamanites into the wilderness.

While the Lamanites were in the wilderness, many of them realized God was giving power to the Nephites. Many Lamanites converted to God.

Some of the Lamanites were Amulonites. They were children of the priests of Noah. When the prophet Abinadi had been burned by Noah, Abinadi told the king: Whatever you do to me will happen to you and your people.

They would not believe. They killed the new believers with fire. Just as Noah's priests burned Abinadi to death, Noah's descendents burned many of their own people.

Abinadi also said they would be scattered and killed like wild beasts kill sheep. When the Lamanites saw the Amulonites had killed some of their own people, they killed many Amulonites and chased the rest into the wilderness. So the words of the prophet Abinadi came true.

The Lamanites would not fight the people of Anti-Nephi-Lehi. They buried their weapons and kept God's commandments. They hoped for salvation and looked forward to the coming of Christ.

Ammon, Aaron, Omner, Himni and their brothers were happy for the success they had with the Lamanites.

Alma 26

Ammon said: My brothers, we have great reason to be happy. When we started, we could not imagine God would give us such great blessings. God made us into his tools to bring thousands of Lamanites into his flock.

Blessed be the name of God. Let us sing to his praise. If we had not come, our Lamanite brothers would still be strangers to God and be full of hatred to us. Now they love him and us.

When Ammon said these words, his brother Aaron scolded him, saying: Ammon, you are bragging. Ammon said: I do not brag on my own strength or my own wisdom.

My joy is full. My heart overflows with joy in my God. I know I am weak. I do not brag about myself; I boast of God. By his strength, I can do all things.

We have done many mighty miracles by his name. Can anyone glory too much in the Lord? Who can say too much about God's great power, mercy and long-suffering? I cannot say the smallest part of what I feel.

Can any natural man know these things? No, only people who repent can know them. Only people who repent and have faith and good works and always pray can know the mysteries of God.

Remember when we told our people in Zarahemla that we were going to the Lamanites? They laughed at us and made fun of us. They said to us: Do you think you can bring Lamanites to the truth? They are a stubborn, evil people. We should kill them before they kill us.

When our hearts were sad and we were about to turn back, the Lord comforted us: Go to your brothers, the Lamanites. Be patient in hardship. I will give you success.

So we trusted in God and went house to house. We taught the people in their homes, in their streets, on their hills and in their churches.

We were thrown out, insulted, spit on and hit in our faces. We have been stoned, tied up and put in prison. We have suffered all kinds of pain and just so we might be able to save one soul.

We thought our joy would be full if we could save a few people. I ask you: Were there only a few? No, they were many. The Lamanites treat us like we were God's angels sent to save them.

If this is bragging, then I brag. This is my life and my light and my salvation. This is my joy and my great thanksgiving. I will give thanks to God forever. Amen.

Alma 27

When the Amalekites saw the Lamanites would not fight, the Amalekites became angry. They began to kill the peaceful people of Anti-Nephi-Lehi.

When Ammon saw the killing among those he so dearly loved, he prayed to God for help. The Lord said: Satan has great hold on the Amalekites. Take the Anti-Nephi-Lehites out of this land.

The people gathered and went to the borders of the Zarahemla. Ammon told the people to stay until he returned. He went to ask permission to bring the people into Zarahemla.

On his way, Ammon met Alma. Ammon's joy was so great

that he fainted. This is a joy given only to the truly repentant, humble seeker of happiness.

Alma led the people of Anti-Nephi-Lehi into Zarahemla. They offered to give them part of their land and protect them from the Amalekites. From that time on, the Anti-Nephi-Lehites became part of the Nephites.

They were known for their love of God and all people. They were perfectly honest. They were firm in their faith in Christ. They would suffer death in the most terrible ways, but they would not fight. They met death without fear.

Alma 28

The Lamanite army followed them to Zarahemla. There was an awful battle. Tens of thousands of Nephites were killed, but the Lamanites were driven out.

This was a time of great sadness among all the people of Nephi. The people's cries for killed husbands and killed fathers and killed sons and killed brothers was heard by everyone. This was a sorrowful day, a time of much fasting and prayer. This ended the fifteenth year of the judges.

Alma 29

O that I were an angel and could have the wish of my heart. I would tell everyone to repent! I would teach every soul to come to God.

But I sin in my wish. I ought to be satisfied with the things the Lord has given me. Why do I want to do more than I am called to do? Why should I wish that I could speak to all the earth?

I do not glory of myself, but I glory in what the Lord has told me to do to bring some soul to repentance. This is my joy. When I see people coming to the Lord God, my soul is filled with joy.

I remember what the Lord has done for me. He hears my prayers. I remember His mercy. When I think of the success of my brothers, my soul is carried away in such great joy that my spirit is separated from my body.

Alma 30

In the seventeenth year, a man named Korihor came into the land of Zarahemla. He told the people that there would be no Christ. He said: No man can know the future. Why do you look for a Christ? These things you call prophecies are just foolish ideas.

You cannot know things you cannot see. You cannot know there will be a Christ. You say you can have forgiveness of your sins. This is crazy. Every person lives by his brains and muscles. Anything a person does is okay.

The high priest Giddonah said to him: Why do you say there will be no Christ? Why do you speak against all the prophecies of the holy prophets?

Korihor said to him: You say those old prophecies are true. I say you do not know they are true. You say that Christ will come. I say you do not know it.

Korihor also argued before Alma. Alma asked him: Do you believe there is a God? He answered: No.

Alma said: I know there is a God and that Christ will come. I know that you believe it, too.

Korihor said: If you will show me a sign that there is a God, I will believe the truth.

Alma said: You have had enough signs. You have the word of all your brothers and all the holy prophets. You have the scriptures. All things show there is a God. The earth and all things on it, and all the planets moving in regular form, show there is a God.

Korihor said: If you show me a sign, then I will admit there is a God. Alma said: I am sad that you fight against the spirit of truth and that your soul will be destroyed. But it is better that your soul is lost than you bring many souls down to destruction by your lying words. If you deny God again, he will take away your voice forever.

Then Korihor said: I do not believe there is a God. Alma said: I give you your sign. In the name of God, you cannot speak.

Then Korihor could no longer speak. Korihor wrote a note, saying: I know I cannot speak and I know only God's power could do this to me. Yes, I always knew there was a God, but the devil tricked me.

Korihor asked Alma to ask God to take the curse away. But Alma said: I know if this curse is taken away you will try again to lead this people away from God.

So, the curse was not taken away. From that time on, Korihor lived by going house to house begging for food and then he died.

Alma 31

Alma learned about a man named Zoram leading people to worship idols. The Nephites feared the Zoramites would join the Lamanites.

Alma knew God's word could lead people to do well. God's word has more power on people than the sword, or anything else.

Alma took teachers to preach to the Zoramites. When they came into the land, they saw the Zoramites had built churches and worshiped in a strange way.

In their churches was a stand high up in the center. Only one person could go on top of it. They called it Rameumptom, which means the holy stand.

A person would climb up in the stand, stretch his hands to the sky and pray: Holy, holy God, we believe you have kept us apart from our childish brothers the Nephites. We believe you have chosen us to be your holy people. You told us there will be

LARRY ANDERSON

no Christ. O God, we thank you we are a chosen and a holy people. Amen.

Every person said the same prayer. After they said the prayer, they went to their homes and never spoke of their God until they returned to the holy stand.

When Alma saw this, his heart was sad. He saw the Zoramites were an evil people. Their hearts were on gold and silver and fancy things. He also saw their hearts were full of pride and bragging.

Alma prayed: O Lord, bless us to bring the Zoramites to Christ. Their souls are precious. Give to us, O Lord, power and wisdom to bring them to you. When Alma said these words, the teachers were filled with the Holy Spirit.

The teachers went separate ways without thinking of what they would eat, or drink, or wear. The Lord gave them food and drink. He gave them strength. When they suffered hardship, they were comforted by the joy of Christ.

Alma 32

Alma taught a large group of poor people on the hill Onidah. One of the people asked him: We are hated because we are poor. Our priests have thrown us out of our churches which we built with our own hands. We have no place to worship our God. What will we do?

When Alma heard this, he was glad. He knew their hardship had humbled them and prepared them to hear God's word. He said to them: You can worship God in other places, too. You should worship every day of the week.

Blessed are you because you have been made humble. Sometimes, if a person is made humble, he will want to repent. Whoever repents will find mercy.

People who become humble and repent because they hear God's word are more blessed than they who are humble only because they are poor.

There are many who say: If you show me a sign from

103

heaven, then we will believe. I ask you, is this faith? No. If a person knows something, he knows it and there is no purpose in believing.

Having faith is not to have a complete knowledge. Faith is hope in things that are true but not yet known. God wants you to believe first, then he will send more of his word to you.

Test my words. Use just a little faith. If you can only want to believe, let this feeling stay until you can believe a little more. Compare God's word to a seed. Make room in your mind and heart for the seed. Do not throw it out by doubting. Give God's Spirit a chance.

If the seed is true, it will begin to grow in your chest. When you feel it beginning to grow, you will say to yourself: This must be a good seed. God's word is good, because it makes my soul grow. My understanding is beginning to grow and be sweet.

Would this increase your faith? I say to you: Yes. But the seed is still small. As the seed begins to grow, you must say: Let us feed it with great care, so it gets roots to grow.

If you neglect the seed, it will not grow roots. When the heat of the sun comes, the seed will shrink away and you will pluck it up and toss it out. This is not because the seed is bad; it is because your ground is dry. You did not feed the seed.

If you will feed God's word by faith and patience, it will grow roots. It will grow into fruit that is sweet above all that is sweet and pure above all that is pure.

Then you will have the rewards of your faith and patience. You will be fed forever.

Alma 33

After Alma spoke, they asked him how to plant God's word in their hearts. Alma said: You have said you could not worship God because you were thrown out of your churches. I say to you, search the scriptures. They teach that we can worship God everywhere, everyday.

Plant God's word in your hearts. Feed it with your faith. It will become a tree of everlasting life. May God make your burdens light, through the joy of his Son. Amen.

Alma 34

Next Amulek began to teach them, saying: We know the question in your minds is if there will be a Christ. I know Christ will come to earth. He will take on him the sins of his people. God has said it.

A payment must be made for our sins, or no one can return to God. The Son of God will make this great payment. Then He will save all who believe in Him.

Use your faith to repent. Pray to God that He will have mercy on you. He is mighty to save. Pray to Him when you are in your fields. Pray to Him in your houses. Pray morning, noon and night. This is not all; you must pour out your souls in your secret places. Even when you are not praying, let your hearts think of God at all times.

After you have done these things, do not turn away the needy. You must visit the sick and share your things. If you do not do these things, your prayers will be wasted.

Now is the time and day of your salvation. This life is the time for men to prepare to meet God. Do not delay the day of your repentance. You cannot say, when you come to your last day, that you will repent and return to God. No, you cannot say this. For the same spirit that rules your bodies when you die will rule you in the eternal world.

Work out your salvation with fear before God. Argue no more against the Holy Ghost. Take on you the name of Christ. Be patient, with a firm hope that you will one day rest from all your troubles.

Alma 35

When Alma and his brothers finished preaching, most of

the Zoramites were angry them. So Alma and his brothers and sons returned to the land of Zarahemla.

The poor Zoramites who believed in God were pushed out of their land. The Nephites gave them land to live in. Alma was sad for the sins of the Zoramites.

Alma 36

Alma gathered his sons together to give them their next duties. He said: My sons, listen to my words. I promise that if you keep God's commandments, you will be blessed. Do as I have done; remember all our people. Help to save them in their hardships.

My son Helaman, you are young; hear my words and learn. Whoever trusts in God will be supported during their troubles. God told me these things by his holy angel when I was younger.

When I was a young man, I went with the sons of Mosiah to destroy the Church. But God sent his holy angel to stop us. He spoke to us with the voice of thunder and the whole earth shook under our feet. I fainted to the ground, because I was afraid he was going to destroy me.

I began to feel awful pain for my terrible sins. The thought of coming to the presence of God made my soul feel terror. For three days and three nights, I suffered for my sins. Then I remembered my father taught me about Jesus Christ, the Son of God, who would pay for the sins of the world. I cried out in my heart: O Jesus, Son of God, have mercy on me.

When I thought this, my pain went away and oh, what joy and wonderful light I did see. My soul was filled with joy as great as my pain! Nothing was as terrible as my pain and nothing was as wonderful and sweet as my joy.

I awoke and stood up. I told the people that I was born again of God. From that time until now, I have worked without stopping to help people repent. I hope for them to taste the great joy I tasted. I hope for them to be born of God and be filled with the Holy Ghost.

My son, the Lord gives me great joy in the fruit of my work. Many souls have been born of God and have tasted his joy. Many have seen eye to eye, as I have.

My son, you should know, as I know, that if you obey God's commandments you will be blessed. If you disobey His commandments, you will be cut off from His presence.

Alma 37

My son Helaman, I command you to take the records. Keep a history of this people, as I have done, on the plates of Nephi. Keep all these things sacred. You may think this is foolishness, but great things are brought to pass by small and simple means.

Teach the people to repent and have faith in the Lord Jesus Christ. Teach them to be humble, meek and lowly in heart. Teach them to never get tired of doing good.

Pray to the Lord in all you do. He will guide you. When you lie down at night, pray to the Lord to watch over you in sleep. When your rise in the morning, let your heart be full of thanks to God. If you do these things, you will be lifted up at the last day.

Now, I have something to say about the special ball-shaped compass our fathers called a Liahona. The Lord made it to show father Lehi the way to the Promised Land.

The Liahona worked for them by faith in God. Just as this compass led our fathers to the Promised Land, the words of Christ will lead you to eternal life.

Do not let the easiness of the way lead you to be lazy. Take care of these sacred things. Go to this people and teach God's word. Be serious. My son, farewell.

Alma 38

My son, Shiblon, you have looked to the Lord your God in your youth. I have had great joy in you already, because of your faithfulness and patience. Be moderate in all things. Be bold, but not pushy.

Control your feelings, so you may be filled with love. Do not pray as the Zoramites; do not say: O God, I thank you that we are better than our brothers. Say instead: O Lord, forgive my unworthiness. Remember my brothers in mercy. Admit your unworthiness before God at all times.

Now go and teach God's word. My son, farewell.

Alma 39

My son, Corianton, I have more to say to you, for you have not had the steadiness of your brother. I do not want to talk about your sins. But you cannot hide your sins from God.

My son, what a great evil you brought on the Zoramites. When they saw your conduct, they would not believe in my words. The Spirit of the Lord says to me: Tell your children to do right or they will lead away the hearts of many people to destruction.

I command you, Corianton, to turn to the Lord with all your mind, might and strength. Do not seek for riches; you cannot take them with you to heaven.

Alma 40

My son, Shiblon, there is a place where spirits live between death and resurrection. When a person dies, the spirit is taken home to God. The spirits of good people go to paradise, a place of happiness, a place of rest and a place of peace. They will rest from all their troubles, cares and sadness. The spirits of evil people go to a place of darkness, crying and grinding of teeth.

Good people stay in paradise; evil people stay in misery until the resurrection. Resurrection is when a person's spirit is brought back into a perfectly healthy body. Not even one hair from your head will be lost.

After the body and spirit join again, good people live in the kingdom of God. Evil people are unclean and no unclean thing can live with God.

Alma 41

Sin never brings happiness. Whatever you send out will return to you joy or sadness.

Alma 42

Let God's justice, mercy and long-suffering control your heart. Let it bring you to humility.

Alma 43

Alma's sons went teaching God's word. Alma, also, could not sit still, so he went with them.

In the eighteenth year of the judges, the Zoramites joined the Lamanites. Zerahemnah was their leader. The leader of the Nephite army was Moroni. He was twenty-five years old. He met the Lamanites in the borders of Jershon. The army of Nephi made breastplates and arm-shields and shields and thick clothing. The soldiers of Zerahemnah were nearly naked.

The Lamanites had many more warriors than the Nephites. Still, the Lamanite soldiers were afraid of the Nephites because of their armor.

The Lamanites ran away into the wilderness of Manti. They did not think Moroni's armies knew where they were going. But Moroni had spies watching their camp. Moroni took most of his army to Manti near the river Sidon. He put half of his men east of the river and half on the west.

As the Lamanites began crossing the river, the work of death began. The Nephite army surrounded them. The Nephites brought death with almost every swing of the sword. Lehi kept his armies on the riverbank so the Lamanites could not come out of the river. Many drowned. Moroni and his army were on the other side of the river. They killed all who came to their side.

The surrounded Lamanites began to fight like dragons. Many Nephites were killed in fierce fighting. The Lamanites' swords split head-plates and pierced deep into the chest. Many arms were cut off. When Moroni's men saw the fierceness and anger of the Lamanites, they were about to run away.

But Moroni inspired their hearts with thoughts of their lands and freedom. The Nephites prayed to the Lord for liberty and freedom.

They began to fight against the Lamanites with power, even though there were only half as many Nephites. The Lamanites became filled with terror. At last, Moroni told his men to stop killing the Lamanites.

Alma 44

Moroni said to Zerahemnah: You are surrounded, but we do not want to kill you. Remember, you attacked us first, but the Lord is with us. You see He has put you in our hands. This has happened because of our faith in Christ and you cannot destroy our faith.

Zerahemnah, I command you in the name of the all-powerful God to give up your weapons. We will spare you if you go away and do not come back to fight us.

If you will not do this, I will send my men to attack and kill every one of you. Then we will see who has power.

Zerahemnah gave up his weapons to the hands of Moroni and said to him: Here are our weapons. We will give them to you, but we will not promise to stay away. It is a promise we know we will break. It is not your God that has put us into your hands. Your armor and shields have protected you.

When Zerahemnah said these words, Moroni returned the sword and weapons and said: We will end this trouble. You will not leave alive unless you promise of peace.

Zerahemnah was angry. He rushed forward to kill Moroni.

As he raised his sword, one of Moroni's soldiers hit it and broke it. He also cut off Zerahemnah's scalp. Zerahemnah ran without his hair back to his soldiers.

The Nephite soldier put Zerahemnah's scalp on the point of his sword and lifted it up. He yelled to the Lamanites: Like the leader's scalp fell to the earth, so will you fall to the earth unless you give up your weapons and give your promise of peace.

Many Lamanites were filled with fear and threw down their weapons at the feet of Moroni. They promised to never fight against the Nephites again. All who did this were allowed to leave into the wilderness.

This made Zerahemnah angry. He tried to get the rest of his soldiers to argue against the Nephites. Moroni became angry about the stubbornness of the Lamanites. He ordered his people to kill them. The Lamanites were quickly being killed by Nephite swords.

When Zerahemnah saw he was about to be killed, he yelled out to Moroni and promised they would never war against them again. So Moroni stopped the work of death. The Lamanites gave up their weapons, made a promise of peace and were allowed to leave.

There were so many dead bodies, they were not counted. The bodies were thrown into the Sidon River and they floated out to the sea.

Alma 45

The people of Nephi were happy because the Lord saved them again. They gave thanks to God. They fasted and prayed much and worshiped God with great joy.

Alma came to his son Helaman and said to him: Do you believe the words I spoke to you about the records that have been kept? Helaman said: Yes, I believe. Alma asked: Do you believe in Jesus Christ? He said: Yes, I believe all the words you spoke. Alma asked again: Will you keep my commandments? Helaman said: Yes, I will keep your commandments with all my heart.

Alma said: You are blessed. I have more to prophesy to you. What I tell you now, you must not tell others. But write the words which I will say. This prophecy will not be made known until after it happens.

These are the words Alma said: Four hundred years after Jesus Christ is crucified, the Lamanites and Nephites will fight until all the Nephites are killed.

After these words were written, Alma blessed his sons; and blessed the people of the church. Then Alma went out of the land. He was never heard from again. Many in the Church thought Alma was taken up to God like Moses.

Alma 46

Helaman taught the people, but many would not listen. Amalickiah, the leader of the unbelievers, was a large, strong man. He wanted to be king. Amalickiah told his people that if they helped to make him king, he would make them rulers over all the people.

Many in the Church began to believe the flattering words of Amalickiah. We see how quickly the people forget God and how quickly they sin.

When Moroni heard of these troubles, he was angry with Amalickiah. Moroni tore his coat and wrote on it: In memory of our God, our religion, our freedom, our peace, our wives and our children. He tied the coat on a pole.

Moroni put on his helmet, his breastplate, his shields and his armor. He bowed himself to the earth and prayed mightily to God. After he prayed, he said: As long as we obey God, he will not allow us to be destroyed.

Moroni went among the people, waving the flag of liberty in the air. The people came running with their armor on and promised they would not abandon the Lord.

Moroni gathered all who wanted to protect their freedom. Amalickiah took his followers and ran away.

Almas 47 to 52

[These Chapters tell about the many wars between the Lamanites and the Nephites. They speak of terrible killing.

Amalickiah joined the Lamanites, killed their leader and took control over their armies. With his brother, Ammoron, he attacked the Nephites many times. Moroni led his armies and his people to fight against them.]

Alma 53

The people of Ammon promised God they would not fight wars again. But they saw the danger and hardships the Nephites suffered for them.

They talked about taking up weapons again. As they were about to make weapons, Helaman convinced them to not break the promise they made to God .

The people of Ammon did have many sons. These sons had not made a promise not to fight. So these young men gathered to help the Nephite soldiers. There were two thousand of these young men who took their weapons to defend their country.

They were all brave. They were young men who were true at all times to God. They were taught to keep God's commandments. Helaman marched at the head of his two thousand stripling (thin) soldiers.

Alma 54

In the twenty-ninth year, Ammoron, the Lamanite leader, sent a request to Moroni to exchange prisoners.

Moroni wrote him, saying: I want to tell you a little about the justice of God and His sword of anger that hangs over you unless you repent and withdraw your armies.

I want to tell you about the awful hell that waits for

murderers like you and your brother. But I think talking to you is useless. I think you are a child of hell.

I will exchange prisoners only if you return one man, his wife and his children for every prisoner I return to you.

If you do not do this, I will come against you with my armies. I will arm our women and children. It will be blood for blood, life for life. I will battle until you are wiped off the face of the earth. Now I close my letter. I am Moroni; I am a leader of the people of the Nephites.

Ammoron read the letter and was angry. He wrote to Moroni saying: I am Ammoron, King of the Lamanites. I do not fear your threats. We are not afraid of you.

I agree to exchange prisoners according to your request, I would rather give food to my own men. Then we will fight an eternal war with you. We know nothing about God and neither do you. If there is such a being, he has made us as well as you.

If there is a devil and a hell, this God will send you to live there with my brother, whom you have hinted has gone to this place. I am Ammoron, a bold Lamanite. I close my letter to Moroni.

Alma 55

When Moroni read the letter, he was even more angry. He said: I will not exchange prisoners with Ammoron. I know the place where the Lamanites guard the prisoners.

Moroni then looked for a Nephite man whose family was Lamanite. They found Laman who had been a servant of the Lamanite king.

Moroni sent Laman and a small number of his men to the Lamanites who guarded the Nephite prisoners. It was in the evening. When they saw him coming, he said to them: Do not fear, I am a Lamanite. We have escaped from the Nephites while they slept and we have wine.

The Lamanite guards greeted him with joy and said to him:

Give us your wine to drink, for we are worn out. Laman said: Let us not drink it now. We should save it until we go to battle.

This made the guards want the wine more. They said: We are worn out. Let us have the wine now. We will get more wine when we go to battle. Laman gave them wine. The wine was strong. The guards soon got drunk and fell asleep.

Moroni had hidden many men just outside the city. While the Lamanites were in a deep, drunken sleep, Moroni's men threw weapons over the walls to the prisoners until they were all armed. All these things were done in a great silence.

When the Lamanites awoke in the morning, they saw the Nephite prisoners had surrounded them. The Lamanite guards surrendered. So without anyone being hurt, Moroni rescued his people.

Alma 56

In the thirtieth year, Moroni received a letter from Helaman, telling about the people in his part of the land. These are the words that Helaman wrote: My dearly beloved brother, Moroni, the two thousand young men that I lead have taken up weapons of war and asked me to be their leader.

In the twenty-sixth year, I marched with these two thousand young men to the city of Judea. I joined my two thousand sons (for they are worthy to be called sons) with the army of Antipus. Many of his soldiers were killed.

When we arrived, I found Antipus and his men working with all their might to protect the city. They were sad in body and in spirit. They fought bravely every day and worked every night to build their forts. They will protect this place or die.

We kept spies out to watch the Lamanite armies. In the second month of this year, many supplies were sent to us from the fathers of my two thousand.

Two thousand more men arrived from the land of Zarahemla. We were prepared with ten thousand men and supplies for them and their wives and children. We hoped the

Lamanites would attack us in our stronghold, but they would not come.

We made a plan. I would march my little sons to a nearby city, as if we were carrying supplies. After we marched from the city, Antipus would follow behind with a part of his army.

My little army came near the city Antiparah, home of the strongest Lamanite army. When their spies told their leader that our little army was near, they marched out with their great army.

We ran away from them to the north. In this way, we led the most powerful army of the Lamanites away from their city.

Then the army of Antipus came upon them from behind. But instead of turning to fight, the Lamanites saw that my little army was small. They thought they could kill us and then escape from Antipus.

I would not allow my little sons to fall into their hands, so we marched quickly to the wilderness. The Lamanites did not dare to stop. I did not dare turn my little sons to the right or to the left for fear that the Lamanites would overtake us and kill us. So all the armies were marching as fast as they could go all day, even until dark.

When the light of morning came, we saw the Lamanites were nearly to us. We ran away from them. They did not chase us far and they halted. We thought Antipus had caught them.

I said to my men: We do not know why they have stopped. It might be a trick to catch us. What do you say, my sons, will you go against them in battle?

Never have I seen so great courage. They said to me: Father, God is with us. He will not allow us to fall. We would not kill if they would let us alone. But let us go, so they do not over-power the army of Antipus.

These little sons, for I call them my sons, never had fought before, yet they did not fear death. They cared more for the liberty of their fathers than they did for their own lives. Their mothers had taught them that if they did not doubt, God would save them. They said: We do not doubt our mothers.

So I marched with my two thousand against the Lamanite

warriors. The armies of Antipus had overtaken them and a terrible battle had begun. But the army of Antipus was tired. They were about to fall into the hands of the Lamanites. If I had not returned with my two thousand, they would have defeated the Nephites. Antipus and many of his leaders were already killed.

The men of Antipus began to run away. The Lamanites were chasing them when I came from behind with my two thousand. These young men began to kill the Lamanites with such great slaughter that the whole army of the Lamanites stopped and turned around.

When the army of Antipus saw that the Lamanites had turned around, they turned also and came back with courage. The armies of Antipus and my two thousand surrounded the Lamanites and we defeated them.

Our brethren fought with God's strength. Never did anyone fight with such power. Their power was so great, they frightened many Lamanite soldiers into surrendering.

When we finished counting and burying the dead, I found to my great joy that not one of my two thousand young stripling warriors was killed.

Alma 57

Ammoron, their king, sent me a letter stating that if I would return the prisoners, he would give back the city of Antiparah. I sent him a letter telling him we had enough men to take the city of Antiparah by force. We prepared to take the city of Antiparah, but the Lamanites of Antiparah ran away without a battle.

We were sent more supplies and six thousand more men and sixty more sons of the Ammonites to join their brothers, my little band of two thousand.

Now that we were strong, we decided to rescue the city Cumeni. We surrounded the city and camped around it for many nights. We captured all the food and supplies that was sent to them. The Lamanites began to lose all hope for help. They, too, gave up the city to us.

But Ammoron sent a large army of men to take back the city. They were about to defeat us. But my little band of two thousand and sixty fought most urgently. They killed all who fought against them. They performed every command with exactness.

I remembered the words their mothers had taught them about having faith in God. We kept our city Cumeni. After the Lamanites ran away, I gave orders to move the wounded from among the dead and dress their wounds.

Out of two thousand and sixty young warriors, two hundred had fainted because of loss of blood. But to our great amazement and joy, not one of these young men was killed or seriously injured. It was amazing to our whole army that all the young men were spared while one thousand of our brothers were killed.

We believe it was the power of God, because of their great faith taught by their mothers. Their mothers taught them there was a just God and whoever did not doubt would be saved by His marvelous power. They are young, their minds are firm and they continually trust in God.

Alma 58

Our next goal was to rescue the city of Manti, but there was no way we could lead the Lamanites out of the city. They remembered what we had done before. We chose to wait for more help and supplies from Zarahemla. I sent a messenger to the governor of our land to inform him of our needs.

While we waited for supplies from Zarahemla, the Lamanites were getting many men and supplies each day. They tried to destroy us many times by tricks. We waited for many months, even until we were about to starve.

We did not know why we were not sent more supplies and men. We began to fear that the judgments of God should come on our people. We poured our souls in prayer to God for Him to strengthen us and save us. The Lord spoke peace to our souls and gave us great faith in Him.

We took our small army against the Lamanites in the city of Manti. I had hidden Gid's men in a place on the right and hid Teomner's men in a place on the left. I kept the rest of my army in front of the Lamanites. When they saw we were not strong, they brought their whole army out. When they almost reached us, I ordered my army to retreat.

The Lamanites chased us with great speed. We led them beyond the hiding places of the men of Gid and Teomner. The men of Gid and Teomner then rose up from their secret places and captured the city.

We turned our march to the land of Zarahemla. When the Lamanites saw we were marching to Zarahemla, they were afraid and began to retreat back.

By now it was night and they pitched their tents. The chief captains of the Lamanites thought they had driven our whole army out of the land. They did not think about the city of Manti. My men did not sleep, but marched at night by another way back to the city of Manti.

On the next day, when the Lamanites returned, they saw we had taken back our city. They were amazed and struck with so much fear they ran away into the wilderness.

So today, we have all our cities. God has given us victory. But we still do not know why the government has not sent us more men and supplies.

This is written late in the twenty-ninth year. My brother, Moroni, may the Lord, our God, favor this people and give you success in rescuing all our lands and people. I am Helaman, the son of Alma.

Alma 59

After Moroni read Helaman's letter, he was happy for their success. Moroni told all his people. But Moroni was angry with the government leaders. He sent a letter to Pahoran, the governor at Zarahemla, asking him to send men and supplies to help the armies of Helaman.

Alma 60

Moroni wrote to Governor Pahoran. These are the words he wrote: I write this letter to Pahoran and to all who have been chosen by the people to manage the affairs of this war. I am upset with you all. You were supposed to arm men and send them to us to battle the Lamanites.

My men and Helaman's men have suffered greatly with hunger, thirst and fatigue. If this were all we had suffered, we would not complain. Thousands have been killed that might not have been killed if you had sent supplies and men. Your neglect has been great.

We want to know why. How can you sit on your thrones in a stupor while your enemies are spreading the work of death around you? They are murdering thousands of your brothers and you have not helped us.

You should have sent armies; you should have sent food. Our men fight and bleed out their lives for you while they starve with hunger.

Unless you repent and send food and men to us and also to Helaman, I will come and stir up revolts against you. I do not fear your power. I only fear God.

I wait for help from you. If you do not send it, I will come to you and kill you with my sword. The Lord said to me: If the leaders do not repent of their sins, you must go to battle against them.

Behold, I am Moroni, your chief captain. I seek not for power, but to pull it down. I seek not for honor of the world, but for the glory of my God and the freedom and welfare of my country. My letter is finished.

Alma 61

Soon after Moroni sent his letter to Pahoran, he received a letter back from him. These are the words he wrote: I, Pahoran, send these words to Moroni. Your great hardships sadden my soul, but there are people here who joy in your troubles. They have rebelled against us. They try to take away the judgment seat.

They keep back your supplies and have threatened our freemen to not come to you. They have driven me out and have taken control of the city of Zarahemla.

They have set up a king over them, named Pachus. He has written to the Lamanites with an offer to join them. I have fled to the land of Gideon with as many men as I could get. I sent a notice throughout this part of the land. The people are flocking to us every day to save their country and their freedom.

In your letter, you have blamed me, but I am not angry. I rejoice in the greatness of your heart. I, Pahoran, do not seek for power, but only to retain my judgment-seat that I may keep the rights and the liberty of my people.

Please, come to me speedily with a few of your men. I have sent a few provisions to you so your army will not die before you can come to me. Gather your force and come here. We will go speedily against the rebels and we will take back the city of Zarahemla. Then we will have more food to send to your armies.

Moroni, I joy in your letter, for I was worried about what to do. I did not know if it would be right to fight against the rebels in our own land. But you said the Lord told you to go against them.

Give strength to Lehi and Teancum. Tell them to fear not, for God will save them and all who stand firm in the liberty God has given them. Now I close my letter to my beloved brother, Moroni.

Alma 62

When Moroni read this letter, his heart took courage and he was filled with joy for Pahoran. Moroni was sad for those who rebelled against their country and their God.

Moroni took a small number of men and marched to the land of Gideon. All along the way, he raised the flag of liberty to gain help. Thousands flocked to him. When Moroni united his forces with Pahoran, they became strong.

Moroni and Pahoran went to Zarahemla and battled against the men of Pachus. Pachus was killed and his men were taken prisoners. Pahoran was restored to his judgment seat.

Moroni immediately sent supplies and an army of six thousand men to Helaman and an army of six thousand men, with food, to the armies of Lehi and Teancum.

Moroni and his army then went from city to city destroying the Lamanite armies until he joined the armies of Lehi and Teancum.

The Lamanite armies were pushed together in one great group in the land of Moroni. Ammoron, the King of the Lamanites, was also with them. Moroni and Lehi and Teancum surrounded them with their armies.

Moroni marched his army on the Lamanites and killed them with an awful slaughter. Those who were not killed were pushed out of the land. This ended the thirty-first year of the judges.

Once more, the people of Nephi had peace. Moroni gave up command of his armies to his son, Moronihah, and retired to his own house to live the rest of his days in peace. Pahoran returned to the governor's seat. Helaman began again to preach the word of God to the people.

Helaman and his brothers taught God's word with much power to the convincing of many people to repent and be baptized. The people of Nephi began to grow strong again. They began to grow rich.

Even though they were rich and strong, they were humble and quick to remember God. They remembered the great things the Lord had done for them. They prayed to the Lord their God continually and the Lord blessed them.

Helaman died, in the thirty-fifth year of the judges. Moroni also died.

Alma 63

In the thirty-seventh year, a large group of people of five thousand and four hundred men, with their wives and children, left the land of Zarahemla and went into the land in the north.

Hagoth was a curious man. He built a large ship and sailed it into the West Sea. In the thirty-eighth year, when the ship returned, Hagoth built other ships. Many more people sailed with him, but they were never heard of again.

Shiblon died and the sacred records were given to his son Helaman. They were handed down from one generation to another.

HELAMAN
Son of Helaman

Helaman 1

After Pahoran died, his sons began to argue about who should be the next governor. Their names were Pahoran, Paanchi and Pacumeni. Pahoran, son of Pahoran, was elected governor over the Nephites. Paanchi and his followers were angry.

They sent Kishkumen in disguise to murder Pahoran as he sat on the governor seat. Pahoran's servants chased Kishkumen, but he was so speedy no one could catch him.

Kishkumen ran back to those who sent him. He made them promise that they would not tell anyone he was the killer. Kishkumen and his group then mixed in with the crowds so they could not be found. Pacumeni was then elected to be governor.

In the forty-first year, the Lamanites had an uncountable army of warriors. They were covered with body armor. Their leader was a large man named Coriantumr. He had once been a Nephite.

The Nephite armies were in the borders of the land. There were not many guards in Zarahemla, because they thought the Lamanites would not dare attack the great city Zarahemla.

Coriantumr marched to Zarahemla with great speed and killed the guards. He brought his army into the city. Pacumeni, the chief judge, ran and was chased and killed by Coriantumr.

Coriantumr then marched to conquer the city of Bountiful. But his march through the center of the land gave Moronihah a chance to bring in his armies. He gave the Lamanites a bloody battle. Coriantumr was killed and the Lamanites surrendered.

Helaman 2

Helaman, the son of Helaman, was elected governor. Kishkumen, who had murdered Pahoran, made a secret plan to kill Helaman, too.

Gadianton was clever in speaking and leading secret murders and robbery. Gadianton convinced them that if they put Kishkumen in the governor seat, he would let them rule others.

One of Helaman's servants learned about the plan. When Kishkumen went to kill Helaman, the servant of Helaman stabbed Kishkumen in the heart; he fell dead without a groan. Gadianton took his gang to the wilderness.

Helaman 3

In the forty-sixth, there was trouble and many arguments. Many people left Zarahemla and went to the north land. They traveled far until they came to large lakes and many rivers. They spread in all parts of the land that had trees.

There were few trees on some parts of the land. The people became skilled at building their houses with cement.

The people began to cover the whole land, from the sea south to the sea north, from the sea west to the sea east. The people in the north lived in tents and houses of cement.

They allowed all the trees to grow up, so they would have trees to build their houses and cities, temples and all kinds of buildings.

Because trees were few in the land northward, much lumber was shipped there. This helped the people in the north build many cities, both of wood and cement.

There was trouble in the south. Helaman kept the laws of the people and the commandments of God, so he was blessed by

God. Helaman had two sons—Nephi and Lehi.

There was peace in the land and great growth in the Church; thousands were baptized, even tens of thousands. God poured out amazing blessings beyond belief.

We see the Lord is merciful to all who will, in sincerity of their hearts, call upon His holy name. Yes, the gate of heaven is open to all who will believe on the name of Jesus Christ, the Son of God. Those who grab on to God's powerful word are in the strait and narrow way that will bring them in the kingdom of heaven.

In the fifty-first year, some pride was in the Church. But the more humble part of the Church fasted and prayed often. They grew stronger and stronger in their humility and firmer and firmer in the faith of Christ. They gave their hearts to God. Their souls were filled with joy and comfort.

Helaman died and his son Nephi began to rule.

Helaman 4

In the fifty-fourth year, there were many arguments and bloodshed in the Church. Some people joined the Lamanites and stirred people up against the Nephites. They captured all of the Nephites' land in the south.

This great loss and death would not have happened if the people had not sinned so much. It was because of pride and riches and because they hurt poor people.

The people did not share their food with the hungry or put clothes on the naked. They hit their humble brothers in their faces. They denied the spirit of prophecy. They lied and stole and murdered. These sins were done by those who claimed to belong to the Church of God. They did not prosper and lost almost all their land.

Moronihah, Nephi and Lehi preached to the people. The people did repent and began to prosper. Moronihah saw they were repenting. So he lead his armies from place to place and city to city until they got back half their lands.

But there were so many Lamanites, it seemed impossible for the Nephites to win back more land. The Nephites were afraid.

They began to remember they had been a stubborn people and had not kept the commandments of God. They lost the Spirit of the Lord. The Lord's Spirit does not stay in unholy places.

Helaman 5

There were more people who chose evil than people who chose good. Helaman told his sons: The devil will send his mighty winds and mighty storms to beat on you; he wants power to drag you down to misery. Obey God's commandments. There is no other way for you to be saved, except by Jesus Christ. Remember Jesus Christ, the Son of God. Remember to build your foundation on Him.

Then Helaman sent his sons to preach from city to city. They preached with great power. God gave them the words to say. Their words amazed the Lamanites and convinced eight thousand to be baptized.

Then the armies of the Lamanites put Nephi and Lehi in prison for many days without food. The soldiers went in the prison to kill them, but Nephi and Lehi were protected by a circle of fire. Nephi and Lehi began to speak, saying: Do not fear. God shows you this wonderful thing.

When they said these words, the earth shook greatly and the walls of the prison shook as if they were about to tumble to the earth. A great darkness came and a voice came, saying: Repent, repent and do not try to kill my servants whom I have sent to you.

When they heard this voice, they noticed it was not a voice of thunder or loud noise, but a still voice of perfect mildness, like a whisper. The voice pierced them to their souls. Even though the voice was mild, it greatly shook the earth and the walls of the prison trembled.

The voice came saying: Repent, repent, the kingdom of

heaven is near. Try no more to kill my servants.

Then the earth shook again and the walls trembled. And the same voice came a third time. The walls trembled again and the earth shook as if it was about to split apart.

The Lamanites were too afraid to move. One of them was a Nephite by birth who had once belonged to the Church of God but had gone away from it. His name was Aminadab. Through the darkness, he saw the faces of Nephi and Lehi. Their faces shined like angels. He saw they were looking up and talking to someone.

Aminadab yelled to the others, about three hundred of them, to turn and look at Nephi and Lehi. They asked: Who are these men talking with? Aminadab said: They are talking with angels.

The Lamanites said: What should we do? Aminadab said to them: You must repent and pray for faith in Christ. They prayed until the dark cloud was gone.

They saw they were encircled by a wall of fire. They were all with Nephi and Lehi in the middle of a flaming fire, but it did not hurt them. They were filled with unspeakable joy.

God's Holy Spirit came down from heaven into their hearts. A pleasant voice like a whisper said: Peace to you because of your faith in my Beloved Son.

When they heard this, they looked up to see where the voice came from. They saw the heavens open. Angels came down out of heaven and blessed them.

The people were told to go and not wonder or doubt. They went and told the things they had seen to all the people. Most of the Lamanites were convinced. The believers laid down their weapons, put away their hatred and gave the Nephites their land back.

Helaman 6

By the end of the sixty-second year, most of the Lamanites

became good. Their goodness was greater than the Nephites. Many of the Nephites were wicked. They rejected the word of God. But the people of the Church had great joy because of the conversion of the Lamanites. They loved one another and had joy together.

Many of the Lamanites came to the land of Zarahemla to tell the Nephites their story of conversion. Many taught with great power and authority.

There was peace, so the people could travel to any part of the land, among the Nephites or the Lamanites. They traded with each other and became rich. They had lots of gold and silver.

The land south became known as Lehi and the land north was called Mulek. There was much gold, silver and precious metals. They raised much grain and many flocks and herds. Their women made all kinds of fine cloth.

But in the sixty-seventh year, the people began to grow wicked again. The Lord had blessed them so long with the riches of the world they began to put their hearts on riches. They tried to be better than each other. They began to commit secret murders and rob to get more riches.

The gang who was formed by Gadianton had many followers. They were called Gadianton's robbers. Most of the Nephites joined this gang. They made secret promises to protect each other. They had secret signs and secret words. They did this so they could murder and steal.

The Nephites grew wicked, while the Lamanites began to grow great in the knowledge of their God. The Lord gave his Spirit to the Lamanites because of their easy willingness to believe in his words.

The Lamanites drove the Gadianton robbers away. But the Nephites built the robbers up so the gang took control of the government. They trampled upon the poor and the meek and the humble followers of God.

Helaman 7

In the sixty-ninth year, Nephi, the son of Helaman, returned from preaching to people in the north land. He saw his people in an awful situation.

The Gadianton robbers were in power. They used their government positions to steal, kill and sin. They punished good people and let the guilty who paid money go free.

When Nephi saw this, his heart swelled with sorrow. He went to a tower in his garden, kneeled down and cried out in agony: Oh, I wish I had lived in the days when father Nephi came from Jerusalem. I would have joy with him in the Promised Land. His people obeyed God. But I know that these are my days and my soul is filled with sorrow because of the wickedness of my brothers.

As Nephi was pouring out his soul to God, certain men passed by and heard him. They ran and told the people what they had seen. People came to learn the reason for Nephi's great sadness. When Nephi arose, he saw the crowds watching him.

He asked: Why have you gathered here? Do you want me to tell you about your sins? You stare and wonder. You have great need to wonder about yourselves. The devil has your hearts. How could you surrender to the devil. He wants to fling you down to misery and endless pain?

You left God to get money and fame. You put your hearts on the useless things of this world. If you do not repent, this great city and all your great cities will be taken away. You will have no place in them.

It will go better for the Lamanites than it will for you unless you repent. They have not had the great knowledge that you have. The Lord will be merciful to them. He will lengthen their days and increase their people. I know these things are true because the Lord told it to me.

Helaman 8

Nephi spoke plainly about their secret sins. When Nephi said these words, some wicked judges got angry. They yelled at him, saying: Grab this man and punish him. Others cried out: Let this man alone. He is a good man. The things he says will surely happen if we do not repent.

Those people who wanted to kill Nephi were afraid to touch him. Nephi began again to speak: My brothers, God gave power to Moses to part the Red Sea. If God gave one man such power, why do you say God has given no power to me? You deny my words and the words of our fathers. They all said the Son of God will come.

Our father Lehi was driven out of Jerusalem because he told of these things. Nephi also testified of these things. Almost all of our fathers, even down to this time, have testified of the coming of Christ.

You have rejected the truth and fought against your holy God. Even now, instead of storing up treasures in heaven, you are piling up sins. Unless you repent, God's anger will come on you soon.

I will give you a sign. Go to the governor seat and search. Your governor, Seezoram, is murdered and he lies in his blood. He was murdered by his brother, who wants to be governor. They both belong to your secret gang.

Helaman 9

When Nephi spoke these words, five of the men ran to the governor-seat. As they ran, they said to each other: Now we can find out if this man is a prophet of God. We do not believe he is, but if the governor is dead, we will believe the other words he spoke.

They ran as fast as they could and came to the governor

seat. They saw the governor was killed and lying in his own blood. They were so amazed, they fainted.

The governor's servants ran and told the people. A crowd gathered at the governor seat. They saw the five men who fainted. They did not know about the words of Nephi. The people thought the five men killed the governor and God stopped them from escaping.

The five men were tied up and the judges asked them what had happened. The five men said: Nephi told us about the murder so we ran to the governor seat. The words of Nephi were true. We were so amazed, we fell to the earth. We do not know who the killer is. We only know we came and the governor was dead.

The judges then yelled out against Nephi, saying: We know Nephi must have planned with someone to kill the governor and then Nephi would tell it. He did this so he could make himself a great man. We will find Nephi and make him confess his crime and tell us who the killer is.

Nephi was tied up and brought to the judges. They said to him: Admit your guilt. We will let you go and give you money if you tell us who the killer is.

Nephi said to them: You fools, you blind people. You ought to howl and cry because of the great death waiting for you, unless you repent.

You say I have planned with a man to murder Seezoram. I will show you another sign. Go to the house of Seantum, the brother of Seezoram. Ask him if I planned with him to kill his brother? He will tell you: No. Then ask him: Did you kill your brother? He will begin to fear and he will not know what to say. He will deny it and act surprised. You will find blood on the edges of his coat.

Ask him: Where did this blood come from? We know it is the blood of your brother. He will start to shake and look pale. Then say: We know you are guilty.

He will confess to you that he killed his brother, the governor. He will tell you that I, Nephi, could only know about his plan by the power of God. Then you will know I am an honest man and that I was sent to you from God.

So they went to Seantum and Nephi's words happened as he said. The five men and Nephi were set free. Some Nephites believed because of Nephi; some believed because of the story told by the five men.

Helaman 10

Nephi walked back toward his house thinking about what the Lord had shown. As he was pondering and feeling much sadness over the people's sins, a voice came to him saying: You are blessed, Nephi. I saw how you gave my words to this people. You did not try to save your own life. You only wanted to know my will and to keep my commandments.

Because you have done this without giving up, I will bless you forever. I will make you mighty. Anything you say will happen, because you do not ask anything against my will.

You are Nephi and I am God. I give you power. Whatever you seal on earth will be sealed in heaven; whatever you loose on earth will be loosed in heaven.

If you say to a building: Be broken in half, it will happen. If you say to a mountain: Be cast down and become smooth, it will happen. If you say God will punish this people, I will punish them. Now I command you to go tell this people that I, the Lord God, who is the Almighty, have said that unless they repent, they will be punished and destroyed.

When the Lord spoke these words, Nephi returned to the people and told them what the Lord said. They yelled at him and tried to capture him. But God's power was with him and they could not hold him.

He was taken away from them by the Spirit. Nephi then went by the power of the Spirit, telling the word of God from group to group until he had told them all.

Helaman 11

For three years things got worse and worse. Nephi prayed to the Lord, saying: Lord, do not allow this people to be destroyed. Let there be a famine in the land to help them remember you. Maybe they will repent .

By the words of Nephi, a famine came; there was little food. The earth was dry and did not grow food for three years. In the more wicked parts of the land, thousands of people died. When the people saw they were about to starve, they began to remember God.

The people began to beg Nephi, saying: We know you are a man of God. Pray to our God to stop this famine.

When Nephi saw the people had repented and were humble, he prayed saying: O Lord, the people do repent. They have swept away the gang from among them. Now, O Lord, because of their humility, will you turn away your anger and stop the famine. O Lord, will you listen to me and let my words happen. Send rain to the earth. Let the earth grow fruit and grain.

The Lord turned his anger away and sent rain and made the fruit and grain grow. The people were so happy.

They gave thanks and glory to God. The people treated Nephi like a great prophet, a man of God having great power and authority. His brother, Lehi, was not a whit behind him as to righteousness.

The Nephites began to grow rich again and spread across the whole land, both in the north and in the south and from the West Sea to the East Sea.

Nephi and Lehi and many of their brothers knew the true gospel. They had revelations daily. So they preached to the people and stopped the arguing.

Some Lamanites murdered and robbed. They would run back into the mountains and their secret places. They became a strong gang of robbers.

Helaman 12

We see how unsteady are the hearts of people. At the time when God blesses his people with flocks and herds, with gold, silver and all things, when he spares their lives and rescues them from their enemies and when he does all things for their happiness, the people harden their hearts and forget God. They trample the Holy One, because of their easy living and great riches.

Unless the Lord gives His people many hardships, unless He visits them with death and with terror and with hunger and thirst, they will not remember Him.

People are foolish, evil, quick to sin and slow to do right. People are quick to put their hearts on the empty things of the world! They are quick to be proud, quick to boast and slow to remember their God. They do not want to be ruled by their God. Blessed are they who will repent and listen to the voice of God.

Helaman 13

A Lamanite, named Samuel, came in the land of Zarahemla and began to preach to the Nephites. The people threw him out. He was going back to his own land, but the voice of the Lord told him to return and preach whatever came to his heart.

So he climbed up on the city wall, stretched his hands out and spoke with a loud voice. He said to the people: I am Samuel, a Lamanite. I speak the words which the Lord puts in my heart. The sword of justice hangs over this people. Terrible destruction will come on this people in less than four hundred years. Nothing can save this people if they do not repent and have faith in the Lord Jesus Christ.

Listen to the words of the Lord. He says you are cursed because of your riches. You have not obeyed Him who gave your riches to you. When a prophet comes and tells you the word of the Lord, you are angry and you try to kill him.

But if a man comes among you saying: There is no sin; do whatever you want, you gladly receive him. You lift him up and you give him gold and fancy clothes, just because he tells you pleasing words. You praise him because he says everything is fine.

Wicked people, the Lord's anger is already growing against you. The time is coming when he will curse your riches. Then you will weep and howl all day and you will say: O, we wish we had repented. O, we wish we had remembered God. O Lord, turn away your anger from us.

But your chances will be past. You will have delayed the day of your salvation until it is too late and your destruction is certain. You have searched all the days of your lives for something you could not have; you search to be happy in sin. O you people, hear my words! Repent and be saved.

Helaman 14

Samuel also said: In five years, God's Son will live on the earth. He will save all people who believe on His name.

I give you a sign of His coming. There will be great lights in heaven. On the night before He comes there will be no darkness. A new star will rise, a star unlike any you have ever seen.

There will be many signs and wonders in heaven. You will all be amazed and wonder. Many of you will faint and fall on the ground.

I have climbed up on the city walls so you might hear and know of the judgments of God which will come on you because of your sins. I come to tell you of the coming of Jesus Christ that you could know the signs of His coming.

Now, I give you a sign of His death. Christ must die so salvation may come. His death will bring the resurrection. His suffering for your sins will bring the chance to repent.

In the day that He will suffer death, the sun will be darkened and there will be no light for three days. While His body lays on the earth without His Spirit, there will be thunder and lightning for many hours. The earth will shake and tremble. Rocks will be broken in two. Those broken rocks will be found ever after all over the earth.

There will be great storms. Mountains will become valleys. Valleys will become mountains. Highways will be broken up. Many cities will be destroyed. Then, by the power of God, He will raise His body back to life.

The purpose of these troubles is to help you believe in God. He gives knowledge to make you free. Remember, remember, you are free. You are permitted to act for yourselves. You can choose life or death. You can do good and be given good, or you can do evil and be given evil.

Helaman 15

You have been a chosen people of the Lord. He has loved the Nephites. He punishes them when they sin. The Lord punishes them because He loves them.

The Lamanites keep God's commandments. All who do this are firm and steadfast in the faith and are made free because of their faith in Christ.

In the latter-days, the Lord's promises will come to our brothers, the Lamanites [American Indians]. Even though they will suffer hardship and be driven, hunted, beaten down and scattered abroad. Even though they will have no place for safety, the Lord will be merciful to them. They will be brought to knowledge of Jesus, their great shepherd.

Helaman 16

Many people heard the words Samuel the Lamanite spoke on the city walls. Those who believed him went and looked for

Nephi to confess their sins and be baptized.

Many people did not believe Samuel. They threw stones at him. Many shot arrows at him as he stood upon the wall. But the Spirit of the Lord was with him, for no one could hit Samuel with stones or arrows. When they saw they could not hit him, many people believed his words.

Nephi was teaching and showing signs and wonders. He did many miracles among the people so they would know Christ would come. He told them things that would soon happen. He baptized those who believed.

Most people did not believe Samuel. When they could not hit him with stones and arrows, they climbed up the city wall to kill him. Samuel jumped down and ran back to his own country. He was never heard of again among the Nephites.

In the ninetieth year, the words of the prophets began to be fulfilled. Angels appeared to tell glad news of great joy. Many great signs were given to the people.

But the people still had hard hearts. The wicked trusted their own strength and wisdom. They said: Those who call themselves prophets are just guessing. We know all these marvelous things cannot happen. It is not reasonable that such a Christ will come. If He does come, why will He not show Himself to us?

Your words are handed down to us by our fathers, to cause us to believe in some strange thing that might happen not here, but in some far away land we cannot know about. We cannot see with our own eyes if this thing is true. You are trying to trick us to make us your slaves.

Thus ended the ninetieth year and Helaman's book.

THIRD NEPHI
Son of Nephi,
and Grandson of Helaman

3rd Nephi 1

Over six hundred years passed since Lehi left Jerusalem. There began to be great signs and miracles. But some people said: The time is passed and the signs spoken by Samuel the prophet have not happened. Your joy and your faith has been wasted.

The people who believed in Christ began to be sad. They watched steadily for the night with no darkness. The unbelievers set a day that all believers would be killed, unless the sign came.

When Nephi saw the evil of his people, his heart was sad. He went out and bowed down and prayed strongly to God all day.

The Lord's voice came to Nephi, saying: Lift your head up and be cheerful. The sign will come tonight. Tomorrow I come into the world. I come to do the Father's will and to show the prophets are true.

That night when the sun went down, there was no darkness. It was as light as noon day. All the people from the west to the east and in the north and south were so amazed they fell to the ground.

They knew the prophets told about this sign for many years. They knew this was the day the Lord would be born. Also, a new star would come in the night.

The people were afraid because of their sins and unbelief. Nephi went among the people baptizing those who repented. Then the people had peace.

The Gadianton robbers, who hid in the mountains, led away many of the Nephite's teenagers to join their gangs.

3rd Nephi 2

The Nephites began to count the years from when the sign came. Nine years passed since the sign of Christ's birth. The people began to be less and less amazed at the signs and wonders from heaven. They began to say miracles were tricks done by men and by the devil.

In the thirteenth year, there were wars and trouble all over the land. The Gadianton robbers grew so much that both the Nephites and the Lamanites had to make weapons to fight them. The war between the robbers and the people became terrible.

3rd Nephi 3

The leader of the robbers sent a letter to Lachoneus, the governor of the Nephites. It said: Lachoneus, most noble governor, I am Giddianhi, governor of the Gadianton people. I write this letter to praise you for your firmness. You stand well, as if you are helped by the hand of a god.

It is a pity you are so foolish to believe you can hold away so many of my brave men. I know they hate you. They are eager to kill you and your people. If we fight you, we will kill you all.

I have written this letter for your safety. Give up. Give up your cities, your lands and your things to my people. If you do not give up, I will send my armies to kill you all.

Lachoneus was a good man and could not be scared by the threats of a robber. So he did not listen to Giddianhi.

Lachoneus called the people to gather together. The people gathered all their horses and chariots and all their flocks and herds and grain. They came by thousands and tens of thousands to one place. They built forts and lived in one group. Lachoneus placed his armies all around them to protect them from the robbers.

Lachoneus told his people they would be saved from the robbers if they repent and pray to the Lord. They feared the words of Lachoneus so much that they repented.

The commander of the armies of the Nephites was Gidgiddoni. The people said to him: Pray to the Lord and let us go battle the robbers in their lands.

Gidgiddoni said to them: The Lord does not allow it. If we go against them, we will lose. We must prepare ourselves in the center of our lands. We will wait until the Lamanites come against us. Then the Lord will put them into our hands.

They prayed to the Lord to save them when the robbers come to kill them. Gidgiddoni had them make weapons of every kind to be strong with armor, shields and bucklers.

3rd Nephi 4

In the eighteenth year, the robbers began to come down from their secret places and take the land and cities left by the Nephites. But there were no animals in those lands for the robbers to eat because the Nephites had burned all the land before they left.

The robbers could not live without stealing food. Giddianhi went to war against the Nephites. Terrible was the day they came to battle. The robbers had painted their bodies in blood and dressed with lambskins around the waist. Their heads were shaved and they wore helmets.

The battle was horrible. There was more killing than any battle before. Their leader Giddianhi fought with boldness, but he was killed. At last, the Nephites pushed the robbers out of the land.

In the twenty first year, the robbers tried to surround the Nephites. But the Nephites marched out by day and by night and killed them by thousands and tens of thousands. Many thousands surrendered. The rest were killed.

The Nephites' hearts were filled with joy. Many cried many

tears of gratitude. The people cried out: Hosanna to the Most High God. Blessed be the name of the Lord God Almighty. They knew they had been saved by God because they had repented and were humble.

3rd Nephi 5

There was not one person among all the Nephites who doubted the holy prophets. They knew Christ had come. They gave up all their sins and served God day and night.

Twenty-five years passed away with many amazing wonders. This book cannot tell even a small part of the great things that happened.

3rd Nephi 6

The Nephites returned to their lands in the twenty-sixth year. Every family took their flocks and herds, horses and cattle and all their things.

They began again to prosper and grow rich. Order and peace was in the land. They formed laws for equality and justice. Now there was nothing to stop them from being blessed, as long as they did not sin.

Many new cities were built; many old cities were repaired. Many roads were made which led from city to city and land to land.

In the twenty-ninth year, there began to be some arguing among the people. Some were lifted up in pride because of their great riches.

There were many lawyers and businessmen and many offi-cers. The people began to be separated by their riches and their chances for learning. Some were not taught because they were poor; others had great learning because they were rich. Some were lifted up in pride and others were humble. Some returned yelling with yelling, while others would be yelled at but would not yell back.

3rd Nephi 7

The people were divided one against another. Nephi boldly told the people to repent. But they became angry with him, because he had greater faith than they. For it was not possible they could disbelieve his words. His faith on the Lord Jesus Christ was so great that angels blessed him every day.

He did many miracles in the name of Jesus. Nephi even brought his brother back to life, after his brother had been killed by the people. The people saw it and they were angry with Nephi because of his righteous power.

Only a few people came to the Lord. Those who repented were visited by the power and Spirit of God, which was in Jesus Christ. All who believed were baptized with water, as a testimony to God and to the people that they repented. God forgave their sins.

3rd Nephi 8

The thirty-third year passed; there was no mistake in the calendar. The people began to look for the sign told by the prophet Samuel. He said that when Christ was killed, there would be three days of darkness.

But the people began to have doubts. They argued about it. In the thirty-fourth year, fourth day of the first month, a great storm arose. The storm was more terrible than anyone had ever seen. The winds were so fast and the thunder was so loud that the whole earth shook. There was sharp lightning, worse than had ever been seen.

The city of Zarahemla caught on fire. The city of Moroni sank into the sea and all its people were drowned. The city of Moronihah was covered with a great mountain. There was even more destruction in the north land. The whole face of the land was changed because of the storm, whirlwinds, thunder, lightning and earthquakes.

The highways were broken up. Many great cities were sunk. Many cities were burned. Many cities were shaken until the buildings fell down and the people inside were killed. Many places were left empty.

Some people were carried away in the whirlwind and no one knows where they went. All these terrible things were done across all the land in about three hours.

Then a thick darkness went across the land. The darkness was so thick that people could feel it like a mist. There could be no light, no candles, no torches and no fire even with dry wood. No light was seen: not the sun, not the moon, not the stars. There was no light at all, not even a glimmer.

The mist of total darkness lasted for three days and three nights. Because of the darkness and destruction, the groaning of the people was terrible. There was great sadness and howling and crying.

The cry was heard: O we should have repented before this terrible day. Then our families would have been spared and they would not have been burned in the great city Zarahemla.

In another place they cried, saying: O if we had only repented and not killed the prophets. Then our mothers, our fair daughters and our children would have been spared. They would not have been buried in the great city Moronihah. The howling of the people was terrifying.

3rd Nephi 9

Then a voice was heard among all the people, saying: Woe, woe, woe to this people; woe to the people of the whole earth unless they repent. For the devil laughs and his angels make merry, because the sons and daughters of my people are killed.

They are killed because of their sins. I have burned up the great city Zarahemla. I have sunk the great city Moroni deep in the sea and its people are drowned.

I have buried the great city Moronihah with earth. I have sunk the cities of Gilgal and Onihah and Mocum deep in the ground and brought water up over them. I sunk the cities of Gadiandi and Gadiomnah and Jacob and Gimgimno deep in the earth.

Their people tried to hide their sins, so I have hidden them from my face. No more will the blood of prophets and saints come up to me against them.

I have burned up the great city Jacobugath because of their evil for their sins were more than all the wickedness of the whole earth. It was they who destroyed the peace of my people and the government of the land.

I burned the city of Laman and the city of Josh and the city of Gad and the city of Kishkumen and all their people, because they cast out the prophets and stoned those I sent to them. I caused terrible destruction on this land and on this people, because of their sins.

You who are alive were spared because you were more righteous than the others. Will you now return to me and repent of your sins so I may heal you? I say to you: if you will come to me, you will have eternal life. My arm of mercy is extended toward you. Whoever will come to me, I will take and bless.

I came to my own, but they did not accept me. Those who receive me, I will make sons and daughters of God. I am the light and the life of the world. I am Alpha and Omega, the beginning and the end.

I am Jesus Christ, the Son of God. I created the heavens and the earth and all things in them. I was with the Father from the beginning. I am in the Father and the Father is in me. The Father glorified His name by me.

I have fulfilled the Law of Moses. Make no more sacrifices of blood or burnt gifts. Give me a humbled heart and a repentant spirit. If you come to me with a broken heart and a contrite spirit, I will baptize you with fire and with the Holy Ghost. I have come to the world to save the world from sin.

Come to me as a little child and I will receive you. I have

laid down my life and I have raised it up again. Repent. Come to me and be saved.

3rd Nephi 10

All the people heard His words. Then there was silence in the land for many hours. People were so amazed, they stopped their sad howling and crying for their lost families.

Then the voice came again to all the people, saying: O you people of these great cities which are destroyed. You are of the house of Israel. How often I tried to gather you like a hen gathers her chickens under her wings. But you would not come to me.

How often I would gather you, if you would only repent and return to me with full purpose of heart. But because you would not repent, your homes and cities were destroyed and your fathers and mothers and brothers and sisters and children were killed. After the people heard these words, they began to weep and howl because of the loss of their families and friends.

The three days of darkness ended. The earth stopped shaking; the rocks stopped breaking. The dreadful groaning stopped and all the awful noises went away.

The weeping and wailing stopped. Sadness turned to joy and praise and thanksgiving to the Lord Jesus Christ, their Savior.

The people who were alive were the more good part of the people. They had received the prophets. They had not shed the blood of the saints.

3rd Nephi 11

A large group of Nephites gathered around the temple in the land Bountiful. They were marveling and wondering about the many changes. They spoke of Jesus Christ and the signs of His death.

They heard a voice from above. They did not know where

the voice came from. It was not a harsh voice; it was not a loud voice. It was a small voice, but it went to their souls. It made their hearts and chests grow and feel hot. It made their whole bodies shake.

They heard the voice again and they still did not understand it. When the voice came the third time, they turned their eyes to the sky where the sound came from. The voice said: Behold my Beloved Son, in whom I am well pleased, in whom I have glorified my name. Hear him.

They saw a man coming down from the sky. He was dressed in a white robe. He came down and stood with the people. The eyes of all the crowd was on Him. They did not dare open their mouths.

At first they thought He was an angel. Then He stretched out His hands and said to the people: I am Jesus Christ, whom the prophets said would come into the world. I am the light and the life of the world. I have done all the Father has asked me to do. I have glorified the Father by taking on me the sins of the world. I have suffered all things for the Father.

When Jesus said these words, all the people fell to the earth. They remembered the prophets had told them Christ would show himself to them after He rose from the dead.

The Lord said: Arise and come to me. Touch your hands on my side. Feel the nail prints in my hands and feet, so you will know I am the God of Israel and of the whole earth. I was killed for the sins of the world.

One by one they put their hands on His side and felt the nail prints in His hands and feet. They knew it was Jesus Christ. When they had all seen, they cried out: Hosanna! Blessed is the name of the Most High God! They kneeled down at the feet of Jesus and worshiped Him.

Jesus called Nephi to come to Him. Nephi came and kissed His feet. The Lord told Nephi to stand and said to Him: I give you power to baptize this people when I am gone back to heaven.

Then the Lord called others and gave them power to baptize. He said to them: Baptize in this way. Take those who repent of their sins down in the water and stand. Call them by name and say: Having authority given me of Jesus Christ, I baptize you in the name of the Father, and of the Son, and of the Holy Ghost. Amen. Then you will lower them under the water and bring them up out of the water. Baptize in this way, in my name.

There should be no arguments among you about my teachings, as there have been. Those who argue are not of me, but are of the devil. For the devil stirs up people's hearts to argue with anger with each other.

Heavenly Father commands all people to repent, believe in me and be baptized. If you do, you will be saved; and you will be given the kingdom of God. Whoever does not believe in me, does not repent and is not baptized, will not go to heaven.

This is my gospel. It comes from Heavenly Father. Whoever believes in me believes in Heavenly Father. And whoever believes in Heavenly Father will believe in me, for the Father and the Holy Ghost and I are one.

Again, I say to you, you must repent, be baptized in my name and become as a little child, or you cannot have the kingdom of God.

This is my way. If you build on my way, you build on my rock and no power can defeat you. Whoever teaches against this is not built on my rock, but built on the sand. When the devil sends his storms and floods, the sandy foundation will crumble down.

Go to people over the land and tell the words I spoke.

3rd Nephi 12

After Jesus spoke these words to His disciples, He stretched out His hand to the crowds and said to them: You are blessed if you follow the words of these twelve men. I have chosen them to serve you and given them power to baptize you. After you are baptized with water, I will send the Holy Ghost to baptize you with fire.

Those who have seen me are blessed if you believe in me and are baptized. Those who have not seen me and believe the words of my servants are even more blessed.

Blessed are the poor in spirit who come to me, for they will have the kingdom of heaven. Blessed are those who are sad, for they will be comforted. Blessed are the meek, for they will be given the earth. Blessed are those who hunger and thirst for goodness, for they will be filled with the Holy Ghost.

Blessed are the merciful, for they will be given mercy. Blessed are the pure in heart, for they will see God. Blessed are the peacemakers. They will be the children of God.

Blessed are you if people hate you or hurt you or lie about you because you believe in me, for you will have great joy in heaven.

I ask you to be the light of this people. Do people light a candle and put it under a bucket? No, but on a candlestick where it gives light to all in the house. Let your light shine so people may see your good works and glorify your Heavenly Father.

Come to me with a humble heart and a repentant spirit. If you will not keep my commandments, you will not enter the kingdom of heaven.

It is written that you must not kill. I say whoever is angry with another person is in danger of God's judgment. Settle your arguments, then come to me with full purpose of heart. I will accept you.

It is written that you must not flirt with another person's husband or wife. I say do not even let bad thoughts enter your heart. It is better for you to resist than go to hell.

It is written, an eye for an eye and a tooth for a tooth. I say you must not try revenge. If someone hits you on your right cheek, turn to him the other cheek. If any person takes away your coat, let him have your cloak also. If a person makes you walk one mile, go with him two.

Give to those who ask you and do not turn away a person who wants to borrow. Agree with your enemy quickly when you are in his way so he will not hurt you.

It is written that you must love your neighbor and hate your enemy. I say to you, love your enemies. Bless those who curse you. Do good to those who hate you. Pray for those who use you and hurt you.

You are all the children of your Father in Heaven. He lets his sun rise on the evil and on the good. Be perfect like me and your Heavenly Father are perfect.

3rd Nephi 13

Help the poor, but do not help them just so you can look good to others. When you help, do not blow a horn before you to get glory. When you help others, do it in secret, then your Heavenly Father will reward you openly.

When you pray, do not pray just so others can see you. Go in your house and shut the door. Pray to your Heavenly Father in secret and he will reward you openly. Do not pray the same words over and over. Your Heavenly Father knows what you need even before you ask.

Pray this way: Our Father who is in heaven, holy is thy name. Let your will be done on earth as it is in heaven. Forgive our debts, as we forgive our debtors. Lead us not into temptation, but rescue us from evil. For yours is the kingdom and the power and the glory, forever. Amen.

If you forgive men their sins, your Heavenly Father will also forgive you. But if you do not forgive others, your Father will not forgive you.

When you fast, do not walk around with a sad face just to show you are fasting.

Do not store treasures on earth, where moth and rust will rot and robbers will steal. Store up treasures in heaven, where robbers cannot come.

Wherever your treasure is, your heart is there also. No one can serve two masters. If he loves one, he will hate the other. If he holds to one, he must let go of the other. You cannot serve both God and riches.

When Jesus spoke these words, he looked at the twelve men He had chosen and said to them: Remember these words. I have chosen you to serve this people. Do not think of your life, or about what you will eat or drink, or wear.

See the birds of the air; your Heavenly Father feeds them. You are much better than birds. If God can dress the grass in the field, he can cover you, if you have faith.

Your Heavenly Father knows what you need. If you seek first the kingdom of God and his desires, then all things will be added to you. Think not of tomorrow; tomorrow will take care of itself.

3rd Nephi 14

Jesus then turned and spoke to the people, saying: Judge not, so you will not be judged. In the same way you judge, God will judge you. Do not see a splinter in your brother's eye, while you ignore a pole in your own eye? You cannot say: Let me pull the splinter out of your eye, while a pole is in your own eye.

Do not give holy things to dogs. Do not throw your pearls to pigs, who trample them under their feet.

Ask and it will be given to you. Seek and you will find. Knock and it will be opened to you. Everyone who asks receives. Everyone who seeks finds.

If a son asks for bread, what father will give a stone? If you know how to give good gifts to your children, how much better gifts your Heavenly Father will give to those who ask Him? Whatever you want people to do to you, do the same to them.

Enter in at the strait gate. Wide is the gate and broad is the way that leads to ruin. Many people go there. Strait is the gate and narrow is the way that leads to eternal life. Few people find it.

Beware of false prophets. They come in sheep's clothing, but they are like wolves inside. You will know them by their actions. A good tree cannot give evil fruit; a bad tree cannot give good fruit.

Not everyone who says to me, Lord, Lord, will come in the kingdom of heaven. Those who do the wishes of my Father in Heaven will come in.

Many will say to me in that day: Lord, Lord, we have said many wonderful things in your name. I will say to them: I never knew you. You did not do as I commanded. Go away from me.

Whoever hears my words and does them is a like a wise person who builds his house on a rock. The rain comes, the floods come and the winds blow and beat on the house. The house stays up because it is built on my rock.

Everyone who hears my words and does not do them is like a foolish person who builds his house on the sand. When the rain and floods come and the winds blow and beat on the house, the house falls down hard.

3rd Nephi 15

Whoever remembers my words and does them, I will raise up at the last day. I am the law and the light. Look to me and endure to the end. I will give eternal life to those who keep my commandments and endure to the end.

Jesus then spoke to his chosen twelve: You are my disciples and you are a light to this people. This is your land and the Father has given it to you. I have not told your brothers in Jerusalem about you or of the other tribes of Israel.

I did tell them that I have other sheep which are not of their flock. I told them that these sheep will also hear my voice. Because of their unbelief, they did not understand. So I was commanded by the Father to say no more to them about you.

You were separated from your brothers in Jerusalem because of their wickedness. Because of their sins, they do not know about you. You are my sheep and the Father has given you to me.

3rd Nephi 16

I also have other sheep that are not in your land or in the land of Jerusalem. They have not heard my voice. I have not shown myself to them at any time. Now the Father commands me to go to them. I go now to show myself.

Write my words after I leave. The words you write will be given to the Gentiles. By the Gentiles, the House of Israel which is scattered across the whole earth will come to know me, their Redeemer.

Then I will gather them in from all the earth. Blessed are the Gentiles, because of their belief in me and in the Holy Ghost. Because of their belief in me, the full truth will come in the latter day to the Gentiles.

Woe to unbelieving Gentiles. They will come to this land [America] and scatter my people [the Indians] who are part of the house of Israel.

The Gentiles will throw your people [the Indians] out from among them. I will let my people [the Indians] be beaten and punished and killed and thrown out and hated and shamed by them.

But the Gentiles will sin and reject the fullness of my gospel. They will lift themselves up in pride above all nations and above all the people of the whole earth.

They will be full of lying, cheating, mischief, hypocrisy, murder, priestcraft and secret groups. This is when I will take my gospel away from them.

I will remember my promise I made to my people. I will bring my gospel to the house of Israel. I will show you, O house of Israel, that the Gentiles will not have power over you. You will learn the fullness of my gospel.

If the Gentiles repent and return to me, they will be a part of the house of Israel. But if they will not repent and listen to my voice, I will allow the house of Israel to go through them and tread them down. The Gentiles will be like salt that has lost its flavor—good for nothing but to be thrown out.

3rd Nephi 17

When Jesus spoke these words, He looked around at the crowd. He said to them: It is time for me to go. I see you are weak. You cannot understand all the words I am commanded by the Father to speak to you today.

Go home and think about the things I said. Pray to the Father, in my name, so you may understand. Prepare your minds. Tomorrow, I come again. Now I will go to the Father. I also go to show myself to the lost tribes of Israel.

Jesus looked around at the people again and saw they were in tears. They looked steadily to Him as if they would ask Him to stay a little longer.

He said to them: My heart is full of love for you. Bring your sick people to me. Bring any who cannot walk. Bring the blind and injured, the leprous and deaf. Bring those who are hurt or sick in any way. I will heal them, for I am full of mercy for you. Your faith is enough that I should heal you.

The people brought all who were hurt or ill and Jesus healed every one. They bowed down at His feet and worshiped him. They came and kissed his feet. Their tears bathed His feet.

Then Jesus told them to bring their little children. The little children sat on the ground around Him. Jesus told the crowd to kneel down on the ground.

Jesus also kneeled. He prayed: Father, I am troubled because of the sins of the people of the house of Israel.

Jesus prayed words to the Father that cannot be written. All the people heard Him. The people said: Our eyes have never seen, and our ears have never heard such great and wonderful things that we saw and heard Jesus speak to the Father. No tongue can speak, nor can there be written by any man, nor can the hearts of men imagine such great and marvelous things we saw and heard Jesus speak.

Our souls were filled with such great joy. People cannot

imagine how great our joy was when we heard Jesus pray for us to the Father.

When Jesus finished praying to the Father, He stood up. But the joy of the people was so great they could not stand. He said to them: Arise. And they arose from the ground. Jesus said to them: You are blessed because of your faith. Now my joy is full.

When He said these words, He cried tears. Then He took their little children one by one and blessed them and prayed to the Father for them. When He finished, He cried again.

Jesus said: See your little ones. Then the heavens opened and angels came down. The angels gathered around the little children and blessed them.

Every person saw it with their own eyes and heard it with their own ears. There were about two thousand five hundred men, women and children.

3rd Nephi 18

Then He told his disciples to get bread and grape juice. He told the people to sit down. He tore the bread into pieces and blessed it. He gave it to his disciples and told them to eat and share it with the people.

When the people were full, He said to the disciples: Ordain one person among you and I will give him power to bless this [sacrament] and give it to all who are baptized into my church. Always do this as I have done: break the bread, bless it and eat it to remember my body that I have shown to you.

This [sacrament] will show Heavenly Father that you always remember me. If you always remember me, you will have my Spirit to be with you.

Then He told His disciples to drink the grape juice and give some to the people. The people drank and were full. Jesus said: The people of my church should always take this [sacrament]. Drink in memory of my blood, which I spilled for you. Do this to show Heavenly Father that you will always remember me. If you always remember me, you will have my Spirit to be with you.

You must watch and pray always. You should pray in my church, as I have prayed among you. Jesus turned again to the crowd and said to them: You must watch and pray always to the Father in my name.

Whatever you ask the Father in my name, which is right, believing that you will receive, will be given to you. Pray in your families to the Father.

Meet together often. Allow all people to come to church; do not put them out. Hold up your light that it may shine to the world. I am the light which you will hold up. I tell none of you to go away, but I invite all to come to me.

Jesus turned to His disciples and said: Do not allow any one to take the sacrament unworthily. If you know a person is unworthy to eat and drink, do not allow it. But do not put him out. Help him and pray for him. If he repents and is baptized, then let him take the sacrament. If he will not repent, he will not be counted among my people.

Even then, do not put him out of the church. Continue to help him, for you do not know if he will repent. If he comes to me with full purpose of heart, I will heal him. Then you will be the tool of bringing salvation to him.

When Jesus ended speaking, He touched His hand on His twelve disciples, one by one, until He had ordained them all. He gave them power to give the Holy Ghost.

The twelve disciples were Nephi and his brother, Timothy, whom Nephi raised from the dead, Jonas, Mathoni, Mathonihah, Kumen, Kumenonhi, Jeremiah, Shemnon, Jonas, Zedekiah and Isaiah.

A cloud came over the crowd. While they were covered by the cloud, Jesus left. The disciples saw Jesus rise to heaven.

3rd Nephi 19

After Jesus left, the people went home. Many people gathered again on the next day. The crowd was so large that the disciples divided them into twelve groups and then taught them.

They told the people to kneel down and pray to the Father in the name of Jesus. The disciples also prayed to the Father in the name of Jesus. They prayed for what they wanted most—the gift of the Holy Ghost.

After they prayed, they went down to the edge of the water. Nephi went into the water and was baptized. Then he baptized the other disciples whom Jesus had chosen. After they were baptized, they were filled with the Holy Ghost.

Angels came down to bless them. Jesus came and stood with them and blessed them. Jesus told them to kneel down and pray.

Jesus then walked a little way off from them and bowed himself to the earth and said: Father, I thank you that you have given the Holy Ghost to these disciples. I have chosen them out of the world because of their faith.

Father, I ask you to give the Holy Ghost to all who believe in their words. Help them believe in me, that I may be in them as you are in me, that we may all be one.

After He prayed to the Father, Jesus came to His disciples. They were still praying. They were filled with hope. The Holy Ghost told them what to pray for.

Jesus smiled on them and the light of His appearance shined on them. They became as bright as Jesus. Their whiteness was brighter than all whiteness. Nothing on earth was so white.

Jesus asked them to keep praying while He walked a little way off and bowed down again. He prayed: Father, I thank you for purifying my chosen disciples, because of their faith. I pray for all who believe on their words, that they may be made pure by me. Father, I do not pray for the world, but for those people you give to me out of the world, because of their faith.

Jesus then came again to His disciples. He saw they were still praying. He smiled on them again, then walked a little way off and prayed to the Father again. The people heard His prayer and their hearts were opened so they could understand. His words were so wonderful and amazing that they cannot be written or spoken by man.

Jesus came again to the disciples and said: I have never seen such great faith among all the Jews. Because of their little faith, I could not show them such great miracles. None of the Jews have seen the great things you have seen. They have not heard the great things you have heard.

3rd Nephi 20

He told the people to keep praying in their hearts. Then He took bread and juice and blessed it for all to eat and drink. No one brought bread or juice, but Jesus truly gave them bread to eat and juice to drink.

Jesus told them: Those who eat this bread, eat of my body for their souls. Those who drink this juice, drink of my blood for their souls. And their souls will never hunger or thirst again.

When all the people ate and drank, they were filled with the Spirit. They cried out, giving glory to Jesus.

3rd Nephi 21

It is wisdom in the Father that the Gentiles are built up in this land [America] and are set up as a free people by the power of the Father. Then these words and promises can come to your people who remain [the Indians]. When they begin to know these things, it will be a sign that the work of the Father has already begun.

In the last days, the Father will do a great and a marvelous work among them. The gospel will be preached among the remainder of this people [the Indians]. The work of the Father will begin among all my scattered people. Then the Father's work will begin among all nations.

3rd Nephi 22

[Jesus repeats the Bible (see Isaiah 54).]

3rd Nephi 23

You ought to search these scriptures. I command you to study the words of Isaiah. He spoke about all the things that will happen to my people.

Jesus said to Nephi: Bring me the record you have kept. You have not written all the things you should have written. I commanded my servant Samuel the Lamanite to tell this people that on the day I rose from the dead many dead saints would come to life.

Then Nephi remembered this thing had not been written. Jesus commanded him to write it on the plates. And it is written.

3rd Nephi 24

Jesus also told them to write the words God gave to Malachi. After they were written, Jesus explained them.

3rd Nephi 25

[Jesus explains prophecies in Malachi 4.]

3rd Nephi 26

Jesus explained all things from the beginning until the time He would come again. He explained things down to the great and last day, when all people will stand before God to be judged.

If they are good, they will have eternal life. If they are evil, they will be cursed, according to the mercy, justice and holiness of Jesus Christ.

The Lord taught the people for three days. Afterwards, He

visited them often and gave them the sacrament. He taught and blessed the children.

The children spoke great and marvelous things to their fathers—greater even than Christ said. Even babies spoke amazing things that, we were not allowed to write down.

They taught and helped each other. They shared all things and were fair with each other. They did all God commanded them.

Not even a hundredth part of the things Jesus taught to the people are written in this book. I, Mormon, a follower of Jesus Christ, God's Son, have written the record of Nephi in this book.

I was going to write all Nephi wrote on other plates, but the Lord told me not to. He said: I will test the faith of my people.

The things I have written are a small part of the things Nephi wrote about Jesus' teachings. I have written these things so they may come some day to the Gentiles and to my people [the Indians]. This book will test their faith. If they believe these things, they will be given even greater things. If they will not believe these things, the greater things will be keep back from them.

3rd Nephi 27

The disciples went and baptized in the name of Jesus. When they met together in mighty prayer and fasting, Jesus came to them again. He said to them: What do you want me to give to you? They said to Him: Lord, we want you to tell us the name of this church. Some people argue about what to call it.

The Lord said: Why argue? Have they read the scriptures that say you must take on you the name of Christ? Do all you do in my name. If it is not called by my name, how can it be my church? If a church is called by Moses' name, then it is Moses' church. So, call the church by my name.

If it is in my name, the Father will hear you. If the church is built on my gospel, the Father will show His works in it. Other churches are not built on my gospel; they are built on the work of men or on the work of the devil. They may have joy for a time, but by and by, the end will come and they will be cut down.

I came into the world to do the will of my Father. My Father sent me to be lifted up on the cross. All people will be lifted up by the Father to stand before me and be judged for their works.

If you repent and be baptized in my name and obey to the end, I will wash away your sins. But those who do not obey to the end will be cut down from the presence of God. No unclean thing can enter into His kingdom. No person will enter into God's peace and rest unless all his sins are washed clean by Jesus Christ. This is my gospel.

You know the things you must do in my church. Do the works you have seen me do. If you do these things, you will be lifted up at the last day.

Write the things you have seen and heard, except those things that are forbidden. Write the works of this people. For this people will be judged out of the books which have been written. All things are written by the Father. What kind of person should you be? Be like me.

I go to the Father now. Whatever you ask from the Father in my name will be given to you. Ask and you will receive. Knock and it will be opened to you. Those who ask will receive.

My joy is full because of you and also this people. Even Heavenly Father and all the holy angels rejoice for this people because none of them are lost.

I am sad about the people who will live. In four generations from now, this people will be led away by the devil. They will sell me for silver, gold and riches. I will visit them then and turn their evil works on their heads.

Jesus said to His disciples: Enter in at the strait gate. Strait is the gate and narrow is the way that leads to life and few will find it. Wide is the gate and broad is the way which leads to death and many people travel there.

3rd Nephi 28

Jesus said to His twelve disciples: Do you want anything from me? Nine of them said: After we finish our missions and lives, we want to come quickly to you in your kingdom.

Jesus answered: You are blessed because you want this thing from me. I promise you, after you are seventy two years old, you will come to me in my kingdom. You will find peace and rest with me.

Jesus then turned to the other three disciples and asked them: What do you want?

They were sad in their hearts, for they did not dare tell Jesus what they wanted. Then he said to them: I know your thoughts. You want the same thing that John, my beloved apostle, wanted from me. You want to live and preach until I return to the earth. You are even more blessed. You will live to see all God's works to the children of men. You will never suffer the pains of death. You will live on earth with no pain or sorrow.

I do this because you want to bring souls to me while this world still stands. For this reason, you will have a fullness of joy. Yes, your joy will be full and you will be like me. I am like the Father and the Father and I are one. The Father sends the Holy Ghost to teach people of the Father and me.

After Jesus spoke these words, He touched the nine disciples with His finger and then He left. The other three disciples were taken away. I, Mormon, was going to write the names of the three disciples who would never taste death, but the Lord stopped me. They are now hidden from the world. I have seen them and they have blessed me.

They will go to the Gentiles and the Gentiles will not know them. They will go among the Jews and the Jews will not know them. They are like angels of God. If they pray to the Father in the name of Jesus, they can show themselves to anyone they choose. They will do great and wonderful things among the Gentiles.

Christ's nine disciples went across the land blessing all the people, baptizing all who believe. Those who were baptized were given the Holy Ghost.

Those who did not belong to the church put the disciples into prison, but the prison walls broke apart. Three times the disciples were thrown into a furnace of fire, but they were not hurt. Twice they were thrown into a den of wild beasts, but they just played with the beasts like children playing with little lambs.

Woe to those who will not listen to the words of Jesus and to His chosen servants. People who do not receive the words of Jesus and His chosen servants will not be received by Jesus at the last day. It would be better for them if they had not been born.

3rd Nephi 29

Some day the Lord will send these words to you. When you see these words coming to you, do not turn away from the Lord. His sword of justice is in His hand.

Woe to anyone who denies Christ and His works! Woe to anyone who denies the revelations of the Lord, or says that the Lord no longer works by revelation, or prophecy, or gifts, or tongues, or healings, or by the power of the Holy Ghost! Woe to anyone who will say that there can be no miracles done by Jesus Christ.

Do not hiss or make fun of Jews or anyone from the house of Israel. The Lord keeps His promises to them.

3rd Nephi 30

Jesus said: O you Gentiles, listen to the words of Jesus Christ, the Son of the living God. Turn from your wicked ways. Repent of your evil works and lying and cheating. Come to me. Be baptized in my name, so your sins may be forgiven and be filled with the Holy Ghost.

FOURTH NEPHI
Son of Nephi

4th Nephi 1

Many years passed with great peace. All the people were baptized to the Lord, both Nephites and Lamanites. There was no trouble and arguments among them. Every person shared all things. There were no rich or poor, slave or free. They were all made free.

The disciples did many wonderful miracles in the name of Jesus Christ. They healed the sick, raised the dead and healed the crippled. The blind could see and the deaf could hear.

The people rebuilt the burned cities—even the great city Zarahemla. They fasted, prayed and met together often to pray and hear the Lord's word. There was no trouble.

Years went by in peace and joy until many of the people who had seen Jesus died. When the disciples chosen by Jesus had all died, except the three who should stay on the earth, other disciples were chosen in their places.

God's love lived in the people's hearts. There was no envy, strife, or lying. Surely there was not a happier people among all the people God created. The people were no longer called Nephites or Lamanites, nor any kind of -ites. They were all the children of Christ.

One hundred ten years had passed and the first generation from Christ had passed away. Nephi wrote his last record and he died. His son Amos wrote history in his place. Amos died and his son Amos kept the record.

Two hundred years passed and the second generation had

all lived and died. The people spread across the land and were rich.

Some people began to be lifted in pride. They wore fancy clothes, fine pearls and costly things. From that time forward, they did not share their things with each other.

They began to be divided into groups and build up different churches to get rich. They began to deny the true church of Christ.

By two hundred ten years, there were many churches in the land. All said they knew Christ the best, but they denied many parts of His gospel. The leaders of one of these churches put the disciples of Jesus into prison. But by the power of God's word, the prison was broke in pieces. The disciples came out and did many mighty miracles.

Still, the people closed their hearts. They were led by greedy priests and false prophets to do all kinds of sins. They beat up the people of Jesus; but the people of Jesus did not fight back.

In the two hundred thirty-first year, there was a great split among the people. The true believers in Christ were called Nephites, Jacobites, Josephites and Zoramites. Those who were against the gospel were called Lamanites, Lemuelites, and Ishmaelites. They fought against the gospel of Christ.

They taught their children to not believe in Jesus and hate the children of God. The Lamanites were taught to hate the Nephites from the beginning.

By the two hundred forty-fourth year, there were more wicked people than good. The Lamanites built fancy churches and covered them with gold and silver and fancy jewels. They had secret gangs like the Gadianton robbers.

The Nephites also began to be proud, because of their great riches. The disciples were sad because of people's sins.

When three hundred years had passed, both the Nephites and the Lamanites were wicked. The robber gangs of Gadianton spread across the land. They put their hearts on gold, silver and saving their treasures. Only the disciples of Jesus were good.

Amos died and his brother, Ammaron, wrote in his place. When three hundred twenty years had passed, the Holy Ghost told Ammaron to hide the sacred records. He hid them so they would later be brought to this people by the Lord.

MORMON

Mormon 1

I, Mormon, write the things I have seen and heard and I call it the Book of Mormon.

When Ammaron hid the records, he came to me. I was ten years old. Ammaron said: I think you are a serious child and quick to watch things. When you are twenty four years old, go to the land Antum to a hill called Shim. I hid there all the sacred writings of this people.

Take the plates of Nephi and leave the others where they are. Write on the plates of Nephi all the things you see happen to this people.

I agreed to do it. When I was eleven years old, my father took me south to the land of Zarahemla. The whole land was covered with buildings and the people were as many as the sands on the seashore.

There was so much sin that the Lord took away his disciples. Miracles stopped. There were no gifts from the Lord and the Holy Ghost did not come.

When I was fifteen years old, I was visited by the Lord. I tasted and knew the goodness of Jesus.

I tried to preach to the people, but the Lord told me to preach no more to them. I lived among them.

The Gadianton robbers spread across the land. The people tried to hide their treasures, but the Lord cursed the land so no one could keep their treasures.

Mormon 2

When I was sixteen years old, the Nephites asked me to lead their armies. The Lamanites came on us with great power. My armies were too scared to fight. They began to run away. The Lamanites chased us to the west seashore.

Even though my people were about to be killed, they would not repent of their sins. Aaron, the Lamanite King, came against us with an army of forty-four thousand. I fought against him with my forty-two thousand. We beat them back.

Because they lost their riches, the Nephites began to cry and howl like the prophet Samuel said they would. Their sadness was not the sadness of repentance. It was the sadness of hopelessness. The Lord would not allow them to always be happy in sin.

They cursed God and wanted to die. Still they fought for their lives. Thousands were killed. Their bodies were piled up like garbage on the land.

My heart was filled with sadness all my days because of their sins. The Nephites were hunted and pushed until we came to the north land called Shem. The power of the Lord was not with us. We were left to our own power. We went against the Lamanites and the robbers until we had won back our lands.

We made a treaty. The Lamanites gave us the land north. We gave the Lamanites the south land. We did not fight again for ten years.

Mormon 3

Then the Lord said to me: Tell this people that if they repent and come to God and build up his church, they will be saved. But the people would not listen.

The Lamanite king sent a letter to me saying his people were preparing to come kill us. I gathered my people to a land called Desolation, near a narrow passage that leads south.

When the Lamanites came, we beat them back to their own lands. They came again the next year and we beat them again. Many of them were killed and thrown into the sea. Our people began to brag about their power. They made an oath to get revenge on the Lamanites.

I, Mormon, refused to be their leader anymore. I had led them into battle many times. I had loved them with all my heart. I had prayed to my God all day long for them. I had saved them three times from the hands of their enemies, but they would not repent.

I now stood as an idle watcher to write the things I saw and heard. I write to you, Gentiles, and also to you, house of Israel. I write to all the people of the earth.

I write to you so you can know you will one day stand before the judgment seat of Christ. All people must stand to be judged for their good and evil works.

I write so you will believe the gospel of Jesus Christ. I wish I could lead you to repent and prepare to stand before the judgment seat of Christ.

Mormon 4

The Nephites went to battle, but they were pushed back. While they were still tired, a fresh army of Lamanites came and killed many of the Nephites. Many were taken prisoner. Some ran away to Teancum by the seashore.

It is impossible to describe the horrible scene of the blood and killing. The people became more evil than ever.

The Nephites were mad because the Lamanites had killed their women and children. The Nephites fought with anger and pushed the Lamanites out.

But from this time on, the Nephites had no power over the Lamanites. The Nephites began to be wiped out like the morning dew is wiped out by the sun.

When I, Mormon, saw the Lamanites were about to win, I went to the hill Shim and dug up the record Ammaron had hidden.

Mormon 5

Then I went with the people. They thought I could save them, so I decided to lead their armies again. But I had no hope. I knew the Lord would punish them, for they would not repent or pray to their God to save them. It was a scene of awful blood and slaughter.

The knowledge of these things must come to the remnant of these people [the Indians] and to the Gentiles [Europeans and Americans]. I speak to them because I know they will feel sorrow for the trouble of the house of Israel. They will feel sadness that this people could have been held in the arms of Jesus.

These things are written and hidden so they will come to you in the Lord's time. This book will go to the unbelieving Jews to teach them that Jesus is the Christ, the Son of the living God.

This book will also help those who remain of this people [the Indians] to more fully believe the gospel of Jesus Christ. It will come to them from the Gentiles.

This people will be scattered and will become a dark, filthy and disgusting people more than any Nephites or Lamanites, because of their unbelief.

Once they were a beautiful people. They had Christ for their shepherd. They were led by God the Father. Now they are led around by Satan, like dust is blown by the wind, or like a ship without a sail or anchor is tossed on the waves.

The Lord will give their blessings to the Gentiles who will come to this land. The Gentiles will scatter and drive them like wild goats.

Then the Lord will remember his promise to the house of Israel. The Lord remembers the prayers of good people. Gentiles, do you know that you are in the hands of God? Do you know that he has all power? Do you know that when God commands, the earth obeys?

Gentiles repent. Humble yourselves before God, or He will come out in justice against you. A part of the people of Jacob will go among you and tear you in pieces like a lion.

Mormon 6

I will now finish writing about the death of my people. In the three hundred eighty-fourth year, I, Mormon, wrote a letter to the Lamanite King asking to let us gather our people who were still alive to the land of Cumorah and meet his people in one final battle. The Lamanite King agreed.

We marched to the land of Cumorah and pitched our tents around the hill Cumorah. It was a land of lakes, rivers and fountains.

I, Mormon, began to be old. I knew this would be the people's last struggle. I hid the plates of Nephi in the hill Cumorah with all the other records, except for a few which I gave to my son Moroni.

One day my people could see the Lamanite armies marching towards them. Every soul was filled with terror because of the greatness of their numbers. The Nephites waited with that awful fear of death that fills the chests of the wicked.

The Lamanites killed my people with their swords, arrows, axes and all kinds of weapons. The ten thousand men who I led were killed. I was wounded, but the Lamanites passed without killing me.

They killed my ten thousand people and Moroni's ten thousand. They killed Gidgiddonah and his ten thousand, Lamah with his ten thousand, Gilgal with his ten thousand, Limhah with his ten thousand, Jeneum with his ten thousand, Cumenihah with his ten thousand, Moronihah with his ten thousand, Antionum with his ten thousand, Shiblom with his ten thousand, Shem with his ten thousand and Josh had with his ten thousand.

Their flesh, bones and blood lay across the land. They were not buried, but were left to rot and mold and crumble to the earth.

Only my son Moroni, twenty-two other Nephites, and I were still alive. A few more escaped into the south land and a few joined the Lamanites.

My soul was low with sadness because of the death of my whole people. I cried out: O you beautiful ones, how could you leave the ways of the Lord! How could you reject Jesus, who stood with open arms to save you!

If you had not done this, you would not have fallen. O you fair sons and daughters, fathers and mothers, husbands and wives, you fair ones, how did you fall?

But you have fallen and I weep for your loss. You are gone and my sorrow cannot bring you back.

The day will soon come when your bodies, which are now molding on the earth, must soon be made perfect and joined with your spirit to stand before the judgment seat of Christ to be judged for your works.

O that you had repented before this great ruin came on you. But you are gone and the Father, yes, the Eternal Father of heaven, knows you and he will do with you according to his justice and mercy.

Mormon 7

Now I speak to the remnant of this people [the Indians]: Do you know that you are of the House of Israel? Do you know that you must also repent? Do you know that you must lay down your weapons of war and delight no more in the shedding of blood?

Do you know that you must come to the knowledge of your fathers and believe in Jesus Christ? He is the Son of God. He has risen from the dead and gained victory over the grave. By the power of Jesus, we will be raised from the dead to stand before God's judgment seat.

By the power of Jesus, we may have our sins washed away to stand before him at the judgment day. By the power of Jesus we can live with God in His kingdom to sing praises to the Father and to the Son and to the Holy Ghost. We can live in happiness that has no end.

Repent and be baptized in the name of Jesus. Grab on to Christ's gospel, which is in this book and also in the other book [Bible], that will come from the Jews.

This book [Book of Mormon] is written to help you believe the other book [Bible]. If you believe that book [Bible], you will believe this book also.

Mormon 8

I am Moroni, son of Mormon. I will finish the record of my father. I have only a few things to write. I will write what my father told me to write.

After the final battle at Cumorah, the Nephites who escaped were hunted down and killed. My father was also killed. They are all dead except me.

I am all alone to write this sad story of my lost people. I do not know if they will kill me. When I am finished writing, I will hide these records in the earth. Then it will not matter where I go.

My father, Mormon, wrote this book. Afterwards, he was killed in battle with all my family. I have no friends left alive. I have no place to go. I do not know how long the Lord will let me live.

Four hundred years have passed away since the birth of our Lord. The Lamanites have hunted the Nephites from city to city and from place to place, until they are all dead. The Lord has allowed it because of their sins.

Now the Lamanites are at war with each other and with the gangs of robbers. The whole land is one constant round of war and murder.

There are none who know the true God. Even the three disciples have been sent out of this land. No one knows where they went, but my father and I have seen them and they have blessed us.

I, Moroni, am the son of Mormon. I am the person who will hide this book in Cumorah. These plates of gold are of no worth to man, because God says no one will have them to get money. But the words are of great worth and the Lord will bless whoever brings them to the world. Blessed is he who brings this book to the world by God's power.

If there are any mistakes in this book, they are the mistakes of a human. Anyone who rejects this book will be in danger of hell fire. Whoever breathes out anger and trouble against the Lord's work is in great danger. Whoever is against the Lord's promised people is in danger of being cut down and thrown into the fire.

The Lord's eternal purposes will roll on until all His promises happen. They will happen in a time when many people will say there are no more miracles. It will come in a time when God's power will be denied. Churches will be lifted up in pride. It will come in a time when leaders of different churches will argue to get more members.

It will come in a time when people hear about fires and storms and smoke in foreign lands. There will be wars, rumors of wars and earthquakes in many places.

It will come when the earth has great pollution. There will be murders, robbing, lying, cheating and all kinds of sins. Many people will say: It is okay to do this or that, because the Lord will say it does not matter. Churches will say: Come to us, we will forgive your sins for your money.

You evil and stubborn people, why do you build up churches to get gain? Why have you changed the holy words of God? Look to the revelations of God; for all these things will happen.

The Lord has shown me great and wonderful things about the last days when these words will come to you. There will only be a few who do not lift themselves up in pride and wear fine clothes. Most will love money, fine clothes and fancy churches more than they love the poor, needy, sick and injured.

Why pollute the holy church of God? Why be ashamed to

take on you the name of Christ? Why dress in clothes that have no life [furs and jewelry] while you let the hungry and sick pass by you without even noticing them?

Why form secret groups to get gain? You cause widows to cry to the Lord and orphans to cry to the Lord for help. God's sword of revenge hangs over you.

Mormon 9

Now I speak to those who do not believe in Christ. When He visits you, will you believe in Him? The Lord will come in great power and glory and you will be brought to stand before Him. Will you then say there is no God?

Will you still deny Christ, the Lamb of God? Do you think you can live with Him in your guilt? Do you think you could be happy to live with holy God when your soul is feeling guilt about breaking His laws?

You would be more miserable living with a holy and just God with your guilt and shame than you would be living with the souls in hell. When you stand before God and Jesus Christ, it will start a fire of shame in you.

Now I speak to those who deny God's revelations and say there are no more prophecies, or gifts, or healing, or speaking with tongues. Those who deny these things do not know the gospel of Christ. God is the same yesterday, today and forever. He does not change. God has not stopped miracles.

Who can understand the amazing works of God? It was a miracle that heaven and earth and people were made by His word. Jesus Christ did many mighty miracles. Also, His apostles did many mighty miracles.

Why would God stop sending miracles? I say to you God does not change. If God stops miracles, it is only because people do not have enough faith.

Now I speak to those who believe in Christ. If you do not doubt, whatever you ask the Father in the name of Christ will be given to you. This promise is to everyone on the earth who believes in Jesus Christ.

Jesus Christ, the Son of God, said to His disciples: Go to the entire world and preach the gospel to every person. Those who believe and are baptized will be saved. Miracles will follow believers.

Who can stand against the works of the Lord? Who can deny His words? Who will rise up against the almighty power of the Lord? All who hate the works of the Lord will wonder and die.

So do not hate and do not wonder. Listen to the words of the Lord and ask the Father in the name of Jesus for whatever you need. Do not doubt. Come to the Lord with all your heart and work out your own salvation with fear and trembling before Him.

Be worthy when you get baptized. Be worthy when you take the sacrament of Christ. Do all things in the name of Jesus Christ, the Son of the living God. If you do this and obey to the end, you will be saved.

I speak to you from the grave. We have written this book in letters that are like Egyptian. The Lord knows that no other people know our language. He will prepare a way for you to understand it.

ETHER

Ether 1

I, Moroni, tell the story of a people who lived here long before the Nephites or Lamanites. Their story is written on twenty-four metal plates. The plates were found by the people of Limhi. It is called the Book of Ether.

Long ago, in the Old Testament land, people built the tower of Babel. The Lord was angry with them. He confused their languages and scattered them over the earth.

One group was lead by Jared. He, his brother, Moriancumer and their families, were near the tower of Babel. Moriancumer was highly favored by the Lord. The Lord had mercy on them and let them keep their language.

The Lord told Moriancumer: Gather your flocks and seeds and your families and friends. I will lead you to a land that is rich above all the lands of the earth. I will make you and your people a great nation. I will do this because of the long time you prayed to me.

Ether 2

They took flocks, birds, fish in barrels and all kinds of seeds. They carried deseret, which means honeybee.

When they came into the north valley, the Lord came down and talked with Moriancumer. The Lord was in a cloud, so Moriancumer could not see him. The Lord told him to take his people into a part of the wilderness where people had never been before.

They walked in the wilderness until the Lord brought them to a great sea. They lived there in tents on the seashore for four years.

One day the Lord came standing in a cloud and talked for three hours with Moriancumer and scolded him because he had not been praying.

Moriancumer repented and prayed to the Lord for his people. The Lord said to him: I will forgive you and your brothers of their sins, but do not sin any more. My Spirit will not always stay with man. If you keep sinning, you will be cut off from me.

The Lord said He would guide them to a great land [America] that is better than all other lands. God had saved this land for a special people.

The Lord told Moriancumer that whoever lived in this land must serve only God, or they would be wiped off the land. It is a choice land and the nation that holds it will be free from all other nations if they will serve Jesus Christ.

The Lord told Moriancumer to build special boats. They were small and light, like a bird sitting on the water. They were built tight like a dish. The ends were peaked and the tops were tight. They were as long as a tree. The doors were tight and there were no windows.

Moriancumer prayed to the Lord, saying: O Lord, we have made eight boats as you explained, but they are so tight there is no light in them. There will be no fresh air to breathe. There is no way to steer.

The Lord said to him: Make a hole in the top and also in the bottom. When you need air, unplug the hole. If water comes in, plug up the hole and use the other hole to get air.

You cannot have windows. They would break in pieces. You cannot take fire with you. You will be like a whale in the sea. The mountain waves will blast on your boats. But I will bring you up from under the sea.

You will not need to steer. I will send winds out of my mouth to blow you where you should go. Your boats will be strong and tight against the waves and winds. What do you want me to do so you will have light when you are under the sea?

Ether 3

Moriancumer found rocks and melted them down into sixteen small stones. The stones were white and clear like glass. He carried them to the top of the mountains and prayed again to the Lord, saying: O Lord, do not be angry because of my weakness. We know you are holy and live in the heavens and that we are unworthy.

But, O Lord, you have told us to ask you for the things we need. Look on us in pity. Do not allow us to go across this raging deep ocean in darkness. I know you have all power and can do anything to help us.

See these stones I have melted of rock; touch them with your finger and make them shine in the dark. We will then have light while we cross the sea. O Lord, will you please do this?

When Moriancumer said these words, the Lord stretched His hand and touched the sixteen stones one by one with His finger. The curtain between heaven and earth was removed. Moriancumer saw the Lord's finger. It looked like the finger of a man. Moriancumer became so afraid that he fell down.

Moriancumer saw the finger of the Lord because of his faith. He knew it was the Lord's finger. Then Moriancumer no longer had faith; he had knowledge. Because of his knowledge, he could not be kept from seeing Jesus.

The Lord said: Arise, why have you fallen? Moriancumer said to the Lord: I saw your finger and I was afraid. I did not know you have a body.

The Lord said: You have seen me because of your faith. Never has any man come with such great faith as you have. Did you see more than my finger? Moriancumer answered: No. Please, Lord, show yourself to me.

The Lord said: Do you believe my words? Moriancumer answered: Yes, Lord, I know you speak the truth. You are a God of truth and you cannot lie.

When he said these words, the Lord showed himself and said: Because you know these things, you are brought back into my presence. I show myself to you.

I am Jesus Christ. I was prepared from the beginning of the world to save my people. Because of me, all mankind will live again after they die. Those who believe in me will become my sons and my daughters. So I am the Father and the Son.

I have never showed myself to any man I created, for never has man believed in me as much as you do. Do you see that you are like me? All people are created in my shape and image. What you see now is my Spirit. One day I will be born on earth in a body with bones and blood.

Because of Moriancumer's great faith, the Lord could not hold anything back from him. So the Lord showed Moriancumer all the people of the earth which had lived and those who would live.

The Lord said to him: Do not tell the things you have seen and heard to the world. Write them in a book and seal them up so no one can read them. You will write them in a language that cannot be read. They will come to the world in my own time.

Ether 4

Moriancumer wrote the things he saw. The Lord commanded that those writings should not come to the people until after he was lifted up on the cross. King Mosiah had kept them secret for this reason, until after Christ showed himself to his people.

I, Moroni, was told by the Lord to write what Moriancumer saw. He told me to seal them. Jesus said to me: These words will not go to the Gentiles [the people in the latter days] until they repent of their sins and become clean before the Lord.

When the Gentiles show faith in me like Moriancumer, I will show them the things I showed Moriancumer. I will unfold all my revelations, says Jesus Christ, the Son of God, the Father of the heavens and of the earth.

People who fight against my word will be cursed. Those who deny these things will be cursed and I will show them no greater things. I am Jesus Christ. My word can open and shut the heavens. My word will shake the earth.

Those who believe my words believe my disciples. If you believe the things I have spoken, I will visit you with my Spirit. Then you will know my words are true.

Whatever teaches you to do right is from me. I lead people to all good. I am the Father, the light and the life and the truth of the world. Come to me and I will show you greater things that are still hidden. Come to me and you will see how great are the things the Father has saved for you from the beginning of the world.

Then you will understand the revelations I gave to my servant John the Revelator. When you see these prophecies, you will know the time is near for these things to happen.

Repent; come to me. Believe in my gospel; be baptized in my name. If you believe and are baptized, you will be saved; but if you do not believe, you will be damned.

Blessed are those who are faithful to my name at the last day; they will be lifted up to live in the kingdom of God. It is I, Jesus Christ, that has said it. Amen.

Ether 5

I write to the person [Joseph Smith, Jr.] who will be lead by the Lord in the last days to these records. Moriancumer's words are sealed shut. Do not touch them; it is not allowed. You may be allowed to show these gold plates to a few persons who help you. Three men will be shown the plates by God's power. They will know these things are true. All things will be established by three witnesses.

Ether 6

I, Moroni, continue telling the story of Jared and his brother, Moriancumer. After the Lord prepared the stones to give light, Moriancumer put one stone in each end of the boats to give light to the boats.

The people prepared all kinds of food for their families and food for their flocks, herds and birds they would carry with them. They went into their boats and went to sea. They put their lives in the hands of the Lord.

The Lord made a great wind blow toward the Promised Land and the boats were moved by the waves of the sea. The boats went under water many times, because of the huge waves and terrible storms caused by the fierce winds.

The great wind never stopped blowing toward the Promised Land. When the boats were under water, water could not come in because the boats were tight like a dish. When they were deep under water, the people prayed to the Lord to bring them up again.

They sang praises to the Lord. Moriancumer sang and thanked the Lord all day. When the night came, they still gave thanks and praise to the Lord.

The boats moved on; nothing could stop them. There always was light, both above the water or under the water. They were on the sea for three hundred forty-four days.

Finally they landed on the Promised Land. When they put their feet on shore, the people bowed down in humility and cried tears of joy, because of the Lord's mercy.

They began to farm the earth. Jared had four sons: Jacom, Gilgah, Mahah and Orihah. Moriancumer also had sons and daughters.

Their twenty two friends also had sons and daughters before they came to the promised land. They began to multiply and spread across the land. They were taught to walk humbly before the Lord.

After some years, Jared and Moriancumer became old. The

people wanted a king. This upset Moriancumer; he said to them: A king will lead to captivity. But Jared said to his brother: Let them have a king. Choose a king from among our sons. They chose the firstborn son of Moriancumer, his name was Pagag. But Pagag refused to be their king. The people asked Moriancumer to command Pagag be their king, but Moriancumer would not force him.

All of Moriancumer's sons were given the chance to be king, but none of them would do it, neither would the sons of Jared, except for Orihah. So Orihah was made king over the people.

King Orihah walked humbly before the Lord. He remembered the great things the Lord had done for them and he taught those things to his people. They were a good people and they began to grow rich.

Jared and Moriancumer died.

Ether 7

All his many years, Orihah ruled fairly. When he died, his son Kib ruled. Corihor, one of Kib's sons, fought against his father and drew away many people after him to live in the land Nehor.

Corihor gathered an army and put his father, the king, in prison. So the words Moriancumer said were true that a king would lead to captivity.

Shule, another of Kib's sons was angry with his brother. Shule made steel swords for the people who supported the king. They battled Corihor and won the kingdom back for his father. Before Kib died, he gave the kingdom to Shule. Shule was fair and good. He spread his kingdom across all the land.

Corihor repented. But Noah, one of Corihor's sons, rebelled against his uncle, Shule, and against his father, Corihor. Noah drew away all his brothers and many of the people and started his own kingdom.

Noah battled Shule and took him captive. The sons of Shule

sneaked into the house of Noah at night and killed him. They broke down the prison door and brought out their father. He ruled again in his kingdom.

During the rule of Shule, the Lord's prophets went among the people and told them to repent from their sins. But the people hated and mocked the prophets.

Shule made a law to allow the prophets to go wherever they wanted. In this way, the people were encouraged to repent. The people repented and the Lord spared them and blessed them.

Ether 8

When Shule died, his son Omer ruled in his place. One of Omer's sons, Jared, battled his father and carried his father away into captivity. Omer was captive half the years of his life. Omer's younger sons, Esrom and Coriantumr, grew up and were angry at their brother Jared. They raised an army to battle him.

They came at night and killed Jared's army. They were about to kill Jared, too, but he begged for mercy.

Jared was sad that he lost his kingdom, for he had put his heart on the glory of the world. Jared had a daughter. She could see his sadness. She was beautiful and smart. She made a plan to win the kingdom for her father.

She asked him: Why are you so sad? Can you not remember the scriptures our fathers brought across the great sea? Those records tell of a group who had secret plans to get kingdoms and great glory.

Father, I am beautiful. Send for Akish, the friend of the king. I will dance for him. I will make him want me. Tell him he can marry me if he brings you the king's head.

When she danced for Akish, he said to Jared: Give her to me for my wife. Jared said: I will give her to you if you will bring me the head of my father, the king.

Akish gathered all Jared's family into the house. He said to them: If I do this, will you promise to not tell? They all promised by their heads they would not tell. They also promised they would kill anyone who did tell.

Ether 9

But the Lord was merciful to the king. He warned king Omer in a dream to leave the land. Omer took his family and traveled many days. They lived by the seashore.

The secret group of Akish and his friends took control of Omer's kingdom. Jared became king and gave his daughter to Akish. But Akish was not content, he went and cut off Jared's head as he sat on his throne.

Akish became king. There was much sin in the land; even his sons tried to kill him. They battled for many years. Nearly all the people of the kingdom killed each other. Only the thirty people in the family of Omer who lived by the seashore were left alive.

In this strange way, Omer came back to an empty throne in an empty kingdom. Omer began to be old; he chose Emer to be king.

The Lord began to take the curse off the land. The kingdom of Emer was blessed for sixty-two years. The people became strong and rich. They had all kinds of fruit, grains, silks and fine cloth. They had gold and silver. They had cattle, oxen, cows, sheep, pigs, goats and many other kinds of animals. They had horses, donkeys and elephants. All useful, especially the elephants.

The Lord poured His blessings on this land—a land better than all others. He said all people who live in the land must serve the Lord, or they would be destroyed.

With good rulers, the people were blessed for many, many years. The people were spread over all the land.

Secret gangs began again. Heth, one of the king's sons, killed his father and took the kingdom. Prophets taught repentance, but the people would not believe their words. Heth let the prophets die in prison without food or water.

The Lord stopped the rain. Many died from hunger and

thirst. Heth starved to death. When the people became humble, the Lord sent rain and there was fruit to eat.

Ether 10

Shez began to build up this broken people. The people began to spread over all the land. Shez lived to an old age. His son Riplakish ruled in his place.

Riplakish was evil. He put too many taxes on the people. He built many big buildings. He built a beautiful throne. He built many prisons to hold the people who would not pay taxes. He forced the people in prison to make gold and fancy things for him. After forty-two years, the people arose and killed Riplakish.

Ether 11

Moroni tells the people's often repeated pattern:
1) First the people repent and are humble.
2) Next the Lord blesses and makes them rich.
3) They have pride.
4) They turn to sin.
5) Then trouble and wars humble the people.
6) Humility helps them repent and be blessed again.
The people repeat this pattern over and over again.

Ether 12

Ether was a prophet of the Lord when Coriantumr was king of all the land. Ether began to prophesy to the people. He preached to the people from morning until the sun went down. He taught the people to believe in God and to repent.

Ether said to them: Those who believe in God can hope for a better world. Faith makes an anchor to the souls of men. Faith will make you sure and steady.

I, Moroni, speak about faith. Faith is to hope for things you have not yet seen. Do not complain if you do not see all things, you will get to see them after your faith has been tested.

It is first by faith that God can do miracles. God has never done any miracles until after people showed their faith in His Son.

It was first by faith that Alma and Amulek made the prison walls fall. It was first by faith that the three disciples were promised they would not taste death.

I know God works with us by our faith. Moriancumer said to the mountain Zerin: Remove. And it was removed.

All the prophets had faith before they did miracles. It was first by our fathers' faith that Christ showed Himself to our people. He did not show Himself to the people until after they had faith in Him.

There were many people whose faith was so strong they could not be kept from seeing into heaven. Moriancumer had such great faith.

When God put out His finger, Moriancumer could see it. After Moriancumer had seen the finger of the Lord, the Lord could not keep anything from his sight.

I, Moroni, have seen Jesus, too. He talked with me face to face and He told me in plain humility about these things.

I have written only a few things He showed me, because of my weakness in writing. The Lord told me to write them, but I said to Him: I am weak in writing. People will make fun of these words. We can only write a little, because of the difficulty in writing on these metal plates. You have not made us mighty in writing like Moriancumer. The things he wrote were mighty like you. His words overpower anyone who reads them.

The Lord answered: If you come to me, I will show you your weakness. I give people weakness so they will be humble. If you humble yourself and have faith in me, I will make your weakness strong. I will show you that faith, hope and charity will bring you back to me.

When I, Moroni, heard these words, I was comforted. I know people must have charity, which is pure love.

Ether 13

Ether saw the days of Christ. Ether told the people about the House of Israel and the land of Jerusalem. He also told them of many wonderful things that would happen in this land [America].

The people treated his words like garbage and threw him out of the city. He hid himself in a cave during the day. At night he secretly watched what happened to the people.

There began to be an awful war. Many people rose up to destroy Coriantumr with secret, evil plans. Coriantumr also knew all the tricks of war.

He would not repent. There were no people on the whole land who would repent. Many people were killed. Even Coriantumr's sons fought much and bled much.

The Lord told Ether: Tell Coriantumr that if he and his people repent, I will spare them. If they do not repent, all his people and family will be destroyed. He will be the last person alive to see the Lord's word come true. Then he will die, too. Coriantumr and his people tried to kill Ether. He ran away and hid in a cave.

A war soon started and Coriantumr took his armies to fight the armies of Shared. They met in great anger and the battle became wild.

Coriantumr killed Shared with his sword. Shared's sword cut Coriantumr's upper leg so that he could not walk well for two years. During this time, all the people on the land were killing each other.

Ether 14

God sent a great curse on the land. If a person put a tool or sword on a shelf, the next day it could not be found. Everyone held tight to their things. No one would share. Every man kept his sword in his hand to fight for his property and his life and for his wives and children.

The wars were so terrible; dead bodies covered the land. The awful stink of death filled the air night and day.

Ether 15

When Coriantumr came back to the war, he was cut deeply many times. Because he lost so much blood, he fainted to the ground. When he woke up, he remembered the words Ether had said to him. Nearly two million of his people had been killed by the sword. Coriantumr began to be sad in his heart. He began to repent, but his soul refused to feel better.

He wrote a letter to Shiz saying that if Shiz would spare the people, Coriantumr would give his kingdom to Shiz. Shiz wrote back saying he would spare the people if he would let Shiz kill him with Coriantumr's own sword.

Instead, they chose to keep fighting. Coriantumr was wounded again and fainted with loss of blood. Coriantumr had his army pitch their tents by the hill Ramah.

Ramah was that same hill that the Nephites later called Cumorah. It was the same hill where the Nephites would later camp before they were killed.

Coriantumr called all the people who were still alive to the hill Ramah. They gathered for four years to get strength for the coming battle. Ether had been watching and writing all the doings of the people.

At last, they all gathered together. All the men, all the women and the children were armed with weapons. They marched to war against each other.

They fought all day until they were too tired to kill each other. When it was night, they went back to their camps and howled and cried all night.

The next day they fought again. When the night came, they filled the air again with their sad cries and howls for their lost ones. The devil had full power over their hearts. They were drunk with anger.

The next morning, they fought all day, and the next day. Only fifty-two of Coriantumr's people were alive and sixty-nine of Shiz's people.

They slept on their swords that night and fought again the next day. When the night came, there were thirty-two people of Shiz and twenty-seven of Coriantumr.

That night they ate and slept and prepared for death.

The next day they fought for three hours. Finally, all were dead except Shiz and Coriantumr.

Shiz arose and yelled in madness that he would kill Coriantumr with his sword or die himself. Coriantumr was leaning on his sword to rest. He fought back and cut off Shiz's head.

Coriantumr now stood alone. All the people had killed each other. He saw that all the words of the Lord had come true. Then Coriantumr fainted and died.

These are the last words written on Ether's record: If the Lord takes me up to Him now, or if He lets me live on alone, it does not matter as long as I am saved in His kingdom. Amen.

MORONI
Son of Mormon

Moroni 1

When I, Moroni, finished writing the story of the Jaredites, I thought I would not write any more. But the Lamanites have not found me. So I am still alive.

The Lamanites are now killing each other. When they find a few Nephites who escaped, the Lamanites kill them, too, if they will not reject Christ. I, Moroni, will not deny Christ, so I wander and hide for safety.

Moroni 2

When Christ was on the earth, He put his hands on His disciples to ordain them. He called them by name and said: Call on the Father in my name in mighty prayer. You will have power to give the Holy Ghost.

Moroni 3

After the disciples prayed, they put their hands on them and said: In the name of Jesus Christ I ordain you a priest, (or, if a teacher, I ordain you to be a teacher) to preach repentance through Jesus Christ and steady faith in Him. Amen.

Moroni 4

Jesus taught the elders and priest to bless bread. They

kneeled down with the Church and prayed to the Father in the name of Christ, saying: O God, the Eternal Father, we ask thee in the name of thy Son, Jesus Christ, to bless and sanctify this bread to the souls of all those who partake of it; that they may eat in remembrance of the body of thy Son, and witness unto thee, O God, the Eternal Father, that they are willing to take upon them the name of thy Son, and always remember Him, and keep His commandments which He hath given them, that they may always have His Spirit to be with them. Amen.

Moroni 5

They blessed the wine juice by kneeling down and saying: O God, the Eternal Father, we ask thee, in the name of thy Son, Jesus Christ, to bless and sanctify this wine to the souls of all those who drink of it, that they may do it in remembrance of the blood of thy Son, which was shed for them; that they may witness unto thee, O God, the Eternal Father, that they do always remember Him, that they may have His Spirit to be with them. Amen.

Moroni 6

I speak now about baptism. People who repented, were humble and wanted to serve Jesus, were baptized. They took on them the name of Christ and their sins were washed clean by the power of the Holy Ghost.

Their names were written down and they were members of the church of Christ. They met together often to fast and pray, to take the sacrament and speak with each other about the happiness of their souls.

Their meetings were guided by the power of the Holy Ghost to preach, teach, pray, or sing.

Moroni 7

I now write a few words my father Mormon taught about faith, hope and charity:

I, Mormon, speak to you by the grace of God the Father and our Lord Jesus Christ. I speak to the peaceable followers of Christ, those who have a good hope that they will enter into the rest of the Lord, from now until they will rest with Him in heaven.

All good comes from God; all bad comes of the devil. The devil is an enemy to God. The devil wants you to sin; God wants you to do good. Everything that invites you to do good, to love God and serve Him comes from God.

Everything that invites people to do good and believe in Christ is from God. Anything that invites men to do evil, to not believe in Christ—and not serve God—comes from the devil.

The Spirit of Christ is given to everyone so they can know good from evil. You should think carefully with the light of Christ so you will know good from evil.

If you will hold on to every good thing, you will be a child of Christ. How is it possible to hold on to every good thing? It is done by faith.

God knows all things and He shows many things to us. He sends angels and prophets to tell about Christ. He shows us heavenly things in many ways.

God sends miracles, angels, prophets, scriptures and the Holy Ghost. These things come by faith.

All these things God shows us helps our faith to grow. Jesus Christ is the source of all good. He said: Ask for any good thing in faith from the Father in my name and it will be done. When you have faith in Christ, you will have hope He can bring you back to God.

This faith and hope will help you to feel grateful and to be careful to obey God. It will help you have love and charity for all people. If you do not have love and charity for others, your faith and hope is wasted. God said that charity, or everlasting love, is the most important thing.

Charity is patience, kindness and joy. When you have charity, you do not want other peoples' things. You will not brag, or become mad easily, or think mean thoughts, or enjoy being bad.

Charity helps you hang on. Charity never fails. Charity is the pure love of Christ and it lasts forever. Whoever has charity, when the last day comes, will be happy. If you have no charity, you have nothing.

Pray to the Father with all the energy of your heart that you will be filled with this love. It is given to all the true followers of Jesus Christ. Those who have faith, hope and charity, will live happily in his kingdom forever. Amen.

Moroni 8

Now, I will tell you the letter that my father, Mormon, wrote to me before he was killed: My beloved son, Moroni, I am happy the Lord Jesus Christ called you to serve Him in His holy work. I think of you always in my prayers.

My son, I write to you about something that brings me sorrow. I have learned there have been arguments among your people about baptizing little children. This mistake should be stopped.

The word of the Lord came to me by the power of the Holy Ghost, saying: Listen to the words of Christ, your Lord and your God. I came into the world to call sinners to repent. Little children cannot sin. They are innocent and clean. I am filled with charity, which is everlasting love, for all children. I love little children with a perfect love.

Moroni, you must teach parents to repent and be baptized and be humble like their little children. But little children do not need to repent. They must not be baptized.

My son, I will write to you again, if I do not have to battle the Lamanites. The pride of the Nephites will bring death unless they repent. Pray for them. Goodbye, my son, until I meet you again. Amen.

Moroni 9

My father wrote me again, saying: My beloved son, I am still alive. I have had a terrible battle with the Lamanites. Archeantus has fallen by the sword and Luram and Emron. Many of our great men have been killed.

Our people will not repent. I think the Lamanites will kill us all. Satan gets them to hate each other. They are so mad that they have no fear of death. They constantly thirst for killing and revenge. The people are cruel and enjoy evil.

The suffering of our women and children is more than I can say. I cannot talk any more about this horrible sight.

But let us work hard. God would be sad if we gave up. We have a duty to do for Him. My son, I trust you will be saved. Be faithful in Christ. I hope to see you again. Amen.

Moroni 10

More than four hundred twenty years have passed away since the birth of Christ. I will soon seal up these records. But first I, Moroni, write to my brothers, the Lamanites [Indians].

When you read these things, think about them in your heart. Ask God, the Eternal Father, in the name of Christ, if these words are true. If you ask with a true heart, with faith in Christ, He will show you by the power of the Holy Ghost that these words are true. And you will know Christ lives and that He is your Savior.

By the power of the Holy Ghost, you can know the truth of all things. So, do not reject the power of God. Do not reject the gifts of God.

God gives some people the gift to teach by the Holy Spirit. He gives other people great faith. He gives some persons the gift of healing. He gives other people power to work mighty miracles. He gives some persons the gift to prophesy about all things.

All these gifts come by the Spirit of Christ. They come to every person according to God's desires. Remember, every good gift comes from Christ.

You must have faith, hope and charity to be saved in God's kingdom. If you do not have hope, you will be in awful sadness. This sadness comes because of sin.

Remember these things. The time will quickly come when you will see me at God's throne. God will say to you: I gave my words to you, written by this man.

God will show you the things I have written are true. So come to Christ and hold on to every good gift. Awake and arise from the dust.

Come to Christ. Resist all evil. Believe in God's word. Be made clean by Christ. In His mercy, He can make you perfect.

I say goodbye to all. I soon go to rest in the paradise of God, until my spirit and body come together again. I will meet you at the pleasing seat of the great Lord Jehovah, the Eternal Judge of all. Amen.

"For feedback or additional information see:
www.BookofMormon.org: